ENERGY, ECOLOGY, ECONOMY

Economic Goods versus Environmental Bads. Intensive industrial development requires a costly complex of facilities to process needed fuels, plus a national transportation net to move them to market. Tankers and pipelines converge on oil refineries at Linden, New Jersey. Refined petroleum leaves this complex, but so do uncontrolled effluents. These render the air malodorous and sometimes unhealthy, and make the Arthur Kill waterway (above) one of the most polluted in the world. (From "Energy and Power" by Chauncey Starr. Copyright © 1971 by Scientific American, Inc. All rights reserved.)

ENERGY, ECOLOGY, ECONOMY

Gerald Garvey

PRINCETON UNIVERSITY

A Project of The Center of International Studies,
Princeton University

W · W · Norton & Company · Inc ·

New York

A Project of The Center of International Studies
Princeton University

All Rights Reserved

Library of Congress Cataloging in Publication Data

Garvey, Gerald, 1935–
    Energy, ecology, economy.

    Includes bibliographical references.
    1.   Environmental policy—United States.   2.   Power
resources—United States.   3.   Pollution—United States.
I.   Title.
HC110.E5G35   301.31'0973   72–5313
ISBN 0–393–05312–1
ISBN 0–393–09408–1 (pbk.)

Published simultaneously in Canada by George J. McLeod
Limited, Toronto

PRINTED IN THE UNITED STATES OF AMERICA
 3 4 5 6 7 8 9 0

This book
is dedicated to
Chip

Contents

▬▬▬▬▬▬▬▬▬▬▬▬▬▬▬▬▬▬▬▬

1. ACCENTING THE POSITIVE   23
   IN WHICH it is argued that America's frontier culture, based on the nineteenth-century belief in the continent's limitless exploitability, fostered patterns of prodigal resource use—patterns which emphasized the positive spillover effects of industrial development, but tended to deny the existence of negative externalities.

2. DEPLETIVE WASTE: AN INTERGENERA-
   TIONAL EXTERNALITY   39
   IN WHICH it is shown that inefficiencies in fuel extraction and conversion entail substantial wastage of energy—wastage which is compounded in the case of electric power—thereby producing an external cost which will be displaced to some future generation, whose forebears' prodigality shall have deprived it of resources.

3. ENERGY AND ECOLOGY   61
   IN WHICH it is shown that market imperfections prevent accurate pecuniary appraisal of environmental externalities, suggesting the need for an "ecological perspective" to evaluate the impact of fuel use in terms of (1) accelerated energy-associated ecosystem aging, and (2) waste build-ups which exceed the ecosystem's capacity to assimilate pollutants.

4. APPALACHIAN RECKONING: THE
   ENVIRONMENTAL COSTS OF COAL   77
   IN WHICH the adverse effects of coal extraction are shown to illustrate a characteristic of energy-associated environmental degradation—"localization of effects" near the sources of ef-

fluents, causing inequitably severe harm to those in the immediate locale.

Figures and Tables

Preface

▄▄▄▄▄▄▄▄▄▄▄▄▄▄▄▄▄▄▄▄▄▄▄▄▄▄▄▄▄▄▄▄

America's frontier culture set a pattern for reckless resource exploitation, often heedless of conservation needs or adverse environmental effects. This study of the environmental impact of energy use in the United States seeks to identify and estimate the major external costs of producing, transporting, and converting fuel. Current and projected consumption patterns for coal, oil, natural gas, nuclear energy, and electric power dramatize the need for a national energy policy. Such a policy should be embedded in a sound, coherent framework of relevant environmental concepts.

No such conceptual framework now exists. Nor does this book pretend altogether to supply the gap. But it does represent, I hope, a useful start.

It is to be emphasized and re-emphasized that my efforts have been mainly conceptual and theoretical, *not* empirical or statistical. The state of quantitative data in the energy-environment field is woeful at best. Nor do the rough-and-ready statistical exercises in the following pages appreciably advance our knowledge on the empirical side. Thus the comparative cost estimates of adverse environmental impacts from fuel use are illustrative only. They are not definitive. The numbers are incomplete. They support the conclusion reached by most scholars working in this area to date—that true cost estimation in such fields as air pollution is an uncertain enterprise at best, and perhaps should be abandoned until supported by an amply funded national effort.

Yet, even after allowing heroic discounts for statistical inadequacies, research suggests that the adverse environmental effects of growing levels of energy use cost society tens of billions of dollars yearly. This figure may be understated, since these effects cannot be fully appraised in dollar terms. Hence energy policy-

13

makers must become sensitized to the ecological as well as to the economic dimensions of fuel use.

It was an awareness of just this need—not my own awareness, but that of policymakers in the Executive Office of the President —which led to this study. I undertook research in June 1969 as a project of Princeton University's Center of International Studies under Contract OST-21 with the Office of Science and Technology in the Executive Office. By agreement with the initiators of the study, Messrs. S. David Freeman and J. Frederick Weinbold, both of OST, research focused on the externalized costs of fuel production and conversion, with emphasis on energy-associated environmental problems. I owe innumerable debts to the OST staff, but would emphasize the independence of my work and my findings. No government office is to be identified in any way with the views expressed herein. My OST friends are most particularly absolved of any responsibility for the policy-oriented sections of the book, especially Chapters 1 and 10. These were drafted after completion of the OST-sponsored research, were supported by private funding, and were not made available even for review by any public official prior to publication.

Where convenient, the sources of statistics are cited in the text itself. In the main, the best sources are government documents published by the U.S. Government Printing Office and available therefrom. Most such studies are brief and well indexed, so specific page references are given only when an interested reader could not readily find the desired data in the cited document. At the end of each chapter a brief reference section is included, designed particularly to annotate quotes or statistics whose source is not made explicit in the text. Finally, an extraordinary freight of data came to these pages from special communications, memoranda, staff studies, and the like. In no case, however, is such information unavailable to the public. An extensive Acknowledgments section follows this Preface, arranged in general to correspond with the chapters and sections on which specific individuals proved most helpful.

This is not, of course, to say that I have always handled all data as fairly or as understandingly as I should have liked. Nor is it to deny that many of the quantitative conclusions take the form of rough extrapolations, "guesstimates," or even informed speculation. I have tried, at least, to minimize the mistakes and explicitly to indicate when the numbers leap from other sources to the realm of personal estimates.

Also, I have tried to present the conceptual framework of the study, and especially the material in Chapter 3, in straightforward terms, with a minimum of jargon and technical abstruseness. An Appendix contains a more formal, mathematical development of the "pollution model" which the text elaborates in qualitative terms. Among other purposes, this Appendix should serve the needs of students or practitioners desiring to fill out the theoretical framework with empirical data. It specifies and formalizes relationships among the main variables in a model which generally applies to various forms of pollution, from strip mine spoil to vented sulfur dioxide, from spilled oil to power plant waste heat.

The Appendix underscores the theoretical, as opposed to the empirical, nature of this book. At the same time, it tries to evidence awareness of the need to complement theory with fact. And it suggests some directions for doing so.

This awareness points up a central theme. Solution of energy-associated environmental problems will take responses that are timely, informed by facts rather than by free enterprise doctrine or "eco-theology," and reliant on a mix of technological and policy adjustments. I hope the following pages support this conclusion on its own merits. I hope too that the conclusion does not spring merely from my own bias. For bias I have.

If any predisposition or prejudice influenced my research and writing, I think, it has been the belief that American society faces a range of critical problems. Some of these problems are probably a good deal more serious than are those of environmental degradation or resource depletion. I doubt that the nation would be well served by doctrinaire preoccupations with the so-called "ecological crisis" at the further expense of already crumbling cities, deteriorating schools, widespread hunger, and unabated race hostility. In an era of environmental ideology of the most dogmatic sort, perhaps such a bias can actually bring to this field a needed—albeit ironic—quality of perspective.

Detroit Lakes, Minnesota, August 15, 1971

Princeton, New Jersey, January 15, 1972

Acknowledgments

▄▄▄▄▄▄▄▄▄▄▄▄▄▄▄▄▄▄▄▄▄▄▄▄▄▄▄▄▄▄▄▄▄▄▄▄▄▄▄

This study profited from many personal contributions by scholarly colleagues, government officials, and industry representatives. Two Princeton students, Neil Griffith and James Paulson, worked closely and imaginatively through the development of both conceptual framework and cost estimates. Their contribution deserves mention—and thanks—at the outset.

In April 1970, a three-day conference on "Energy and Environment" was sponsored at Princeton's Woodrow Wilson School by the university's Center of International Studies and the Office of Science and Technology, Executive Office of the President. The participants reviewed the initial phase of research for this volume. Many attendees made extremely helpful suggestions. Present were Lee DuBridge, then Science Advisor to the President, plus S. David Freeman, J. Frederick Weinhold, and Milton Searl from the OST staff. Other federal officials were John Ludwig, Associate Commissioner, National Air Pollution Control Administration; John Ford, White House Staff; James Ramey, Atomic Energy Commissioner; and Haskell Wald, Chief Economist, Federal Power Commission. Participants from the academic community included: William Capron of the Harvard Kennedy School; Hans Landsberg of Resources for the Future; Lawrence Hinkle, M.D. of Cornell Medical School; Mancur Olson of the University of Maryland; and from Princeton University, Robert Axtmann, Cyril Black, Harold Feiveson, Robert Gilpin, Melvin Gottlieb, Lyman Spitzer, Harold Sprout, John Tukey, and myself. Mr. Michael Core attended as a representative of the American Academy for the Advancement of Science.

Other colleagues and students who have helped, either by furnishing expertise or by critiquing portions of the study, are:

16

Henry Abarbanel and Marvin Goldberger of the Princeton Physics Department; Wallace Oates of the Princeton Economics Department; Terry Davies and Keith Pavett, during their tenures as faculty members of the Woodrow Wilson school; Jack Gibbons of Oak Ridge National Laboratory's Environmental Studies Group; and James Brown, Gray Ellrodt (who conducted on-site research on the effects of the Santa Barbara oil spill), Billy Groos, Kenneth Jacobson, Tony Lasaga, David MacMahon, Bruce Nickerson, Albert Opp, and William Travers. My colleagues Duane Lockard (Politics), George Reynolds (Physics), and Robert Socolow (Engineering) read earlier drafts of the study in full. Their suggestions were uniformly helpful—and much appreciated. Acknowledgments are also due to Mrs. Bernis Terry of Princeton and Mrs. Norman Eilertson of Detroit Lakes, Minnesota, for efforts far "above and beyond the call" as typists.

Special thanks are owed David Eaton, staff member, Environmental Quality Council; Henry Horn of Princeton's Biology Department; and my friend Bruce Nickerson for their critical readings of earlier drafts of Chapters 2 and 3. Appreciation—and explicit exoneration of any errors which remain—are due too to William Capron of Harvard, who gave these sections a close (not to say hostile) critique.

Others who reviewed all or part of Chapter 2, and who deserve particular thanks, are: J. E. Hodge, Director of the Statistics and Economics Division, American Petroleum Institute; Robert Axtmann and William Travers of Princeton's Engineering School and Geology Departments; Ralph Johnson and Haskell Wald of FPC's Office of Economics; and Zane Murphy of the Bureau of Mines, Interior Department.

Special thanks are due Aubrey Wagner and Paul Evans, the Chairman and the Information Director of TVA, for providing much background material drawn on throughout Chapter 4, and indeed throughout the study. The TVA staff reviewed the penultimate draft of the section on coal and made many helpful suggestions. Mr. Evans also furnished the report by James Boyer, cited in the text, and the range of cost figures used to supplement Interior Department estimates of land reclamation expenses. Zane Murphy, Acting Chief in the Coal Branch of the

Bureau of Mines Fossil Fuel Division, read this chapter and provided many corrections of detail. Finally, through the good offices of Mrs. Betsy Kraft, National Coal Association, members of the NCA staff reviewed the penultimate draft of Chapter 4 and offered helpful suggestions.

Personal thanks in connection with the preparation of Chapter 5 are due to Russell G. Wayland, Chief of Conservation Division, U.S. Geological Survey; Edmond H. Farrington, Assistant Director, National Petroleum Council; Harry Perry, Senior Specialist in the L. C. Environmental Policy Division; William Travers, Geology Department, Cornell University—each of whom gave much help, including critical review of relevant parts of the manuscript. John Hodges, American Petroleum Institute, deserves special thanks for having API staff members give a detailed reading of the penultimate draft of Chapter 5.

For general quantitative ecological estimates of oil spill damage, see M. Blumer *et. al.*, "The West Falmouth Oil Spill," Woods Hole #70–44, September, 1970; M. Blumer *et. al.*, "Hydrocarbon Pollution of Edible Shellfish by an Oil Spill," 5 *Marine Biology* 195; and M. Blumer, "Oil Contamination and the Living Resources of the Sea," Woods Hole Contribution #2474. In a personal communication, Dr. Blumer also furnished the cost figures for the West Falmouth spill damage settlements.

Oil spillage estimates are based on U.S. Coast Guard reports provided by Cmdr. Daniel Charter, Chief, Environmental Coordination Branch. This office was extraordinarily helpful and responsive, and several of its members reviewed and critiqued the relevant sections of Chapter 5. Mr. Melvin Judah, Chief of Industry Programs in the Office of Pipeline Safety provided statistical data and reviewed the relevant portion of the draft.

A massive study by the Research Triangle Institute, "Comprehensive Study of Specified Air Pollution Sources to Assess the Economic Effects of Air Quality Standards," gives background to the cost issues treated in Chapter 6. This study by D. A. LeSourd *et. al.*, reported December 1970, was made available through the courtesy of Paul Gearhardt of the Environmental Protection Agency. Appreciation is also extended for help on this chapter to Fred Lawrence, an air pollution specialist with the Environmental Protection Agency, and John Ludwig, Acting

Chief for Air Pollution of EPA's Science and Technology Division, both of whom reviewed the penultimate draft of Chapter 6 and offered many useful (and used!) suggestions; Larry Milasc of the New Jersey Motor Vehicle Control Office, Department of Environmental Quality; Dr. Terry Davies of the Council on Environmental Quality Staff; Dr. David Rose of MIT and Oak Ridge National Laboratory; and Allen Kneese of Resources for the Future, whose "How Much Is Air Pollution Costing Us?," delivered at the 1966 National Conference on Air Pollution in Washington, D.C. remains a most hard-headed set of non-conclusions in this "will o'wispy" area.

On nuclear health effects, a paper kindly furnished by my colleague Herman Somers, "Atomic Energy and Workmen's Compensation," presented before the Pacific Coast Metal Trades Council Conference, May 1957, Long Beach, remains a lucid statement of general principles. Special thanks are due John Gofman of the Lawrence Radiation Laboratory for personal communications, including a review of Chapter 7 in draft and several detailed papers on the Gofman-Tamplin hypothesis; and to Joshua Lederberg for personal communications, including both published and unpublished analyses of the genetic danger. These most helpful correspondents are, of course, specifically exempted from any blame for errors of fact or judgment that remain in the text.

Chapter 8 could not have been completed without the extensive assistance of Milton Shaw, Director of the AEC Division of Reactor Development and Technology. Particularly helpful were personal communications detailing the AEC position on reactor safety. W. H. McVey and his staff, and all of Mr. Shaw's staff, gave a line-by-line review of Chapter 6 and provided nine pages of detailed annotations and challenges. Many of these comments proved useful, and the entire exercise was a constructive one.

Thanks are also due Craig Sinclair, Senior Research Fellow of the University of Sussex Science Policy Research Unit, England, and a specialist in nuclear safety, for rewarding and relevant personal conversation, as well as for useful data extracted from British sources. For various help and kindnesses, thanks are also expressed to Mr. John F. Smith of Wood, Struthers and Winthrop in New York City, and to Robert Axtmann, who subjected the whole of Chapter 7 to a challenging critique.

For Chapter 8, personal communications from Henry Horn of Princeton's Biology Department have been invaluable, as has the extensive help—including a paragraph-by-paragraph critique of an earlier draft—given by Joseph H. Caldwell, Chief of Engineering, Civil Works Directorate of the Corps of Engineers. Thanks are expressed, again, to Robert Axtmann of Princeton for reviewing an earlier version of Chapter 8, and also to J. B. Burnbaum of Battelle Institute for forwarding three extremely useful studies of thermal effects.

On the electric power industry in general, William Webb, Director of FPC's Information Office, gave freely of his time and provided copies of all pertinent statistical publications. Oran L. Culberson of the University of Tennessee, a participant in Oak Ridge National Laboratory's Environmental Study Task Force, shared valuable unpublished statistical data from his research on electric power consumption patterns.

The greatest thanks of all are due my wife Lou Ann.

ENERGY, ECOLOGY, ECONOMY

A Clear-Cut Nineteenth-Century Wisconsin Forest. Reckless harvesting of the continent's forests—America's first major energy source—set the pattern for subsequent exploitation of fuel resources. (Reprinted by permission of the State Historical Society of Wisconsin.)

. . . we have in general permitted economic activities without assessing the operator for their adverse effects. There has been no attempt to evaluate—and to charge for—externalities. As Boulding says, we pay people for the goods they produce, but do not make them pay for the bads.

Ansley J. Coale,
170 *Science* 132

1

Accenting the Positive

~~~~~~~~~~~~~~~~~~~~~~~~~~~~~~~~~~~~

Fuel is needed to make anything go. A living organism feeds on fuel in the form of food. A car or a plane burns refined oil. For the economy at large, energy is literally the propellant, just as coal and oil and electric power are physical prerequisites, of growth in a modern society.

In an expanding economy, demand for energy becomes "an appetite that grows by what it feeds on." As a result, energy use tends to outstrip other main indicators of expansion, such as population growth and increases in Gross National Product. Between 1960 and 1968, for example, population increased by 11% while total energy consumption jumped 39%. Demand for aircraft fuel more than tripled between 1960 and 1970. Energy use by electric utilities almost doubled in the same period.

The adverse effects of cascading energy use also tend to accu-

mulate at an accelerating rate. These effects include waste of resources in a society fabled for its prodigality. A growing pollution problem is associated with raw fuel production from mines
and oil- or gas-wells. The conversion of fossil or nuclear fuels at
the consumption end adds to the weight of residues for assimilation by the environment.

Thus energy as an essential economic "good" in modern
American society must be balanced against certain "bads" associated with fuel use. The existence of these bads gives rise to the
environmental problem.

Current ecological issues cannot be understood, let alone
dealt with, except with a view to inherited American attitudes.
These attitudes threaten to propel history's most richly endowed
society toward environmental impoverishment. America's tradition of resource exploitation illuminates the tension between energy use and environmental quality. The energy-environment
problem is historical in nature—rooted in practices that were
suitable to a less urbanized society, to the simpler economy of
frontier America. With history, then, environmental analysis
properly begins.

Private Practice and Public Policy:
The Frontier Style

A questioner once asked Franklin D. Roosevelt what one book
above all others the then President would like every citizen of
the Soviet Union to read. Ignoring the recognized scriptures of
democratic philosophy, FDR quickly replied: "The Sears, Roe-
buck catalogue!" The anecdote rings true. FDR's answer combined two characteristics of the American tradition. First, it emphasized economic factors over philosophical and political
concerns. Second, it revealed a sturdy recognition of the continent's material richness, diversity, and productive potential as
the decisive elements in America's story.

To subdue this material potential became the dominant aspiration of American frontiersmen. To help achieve this aspiration,
there developed certain traits of culture that survived the early
twentieth-century passing of the frontier.

The frontier culture helped form the American character. It

still shapes his natural resource policies. The seemingly limitless bounty of the continent fostered reckless, wasteful habits, first manifested in the frontiersman's appropriation of land and forests, then carried over into the eras of coal and petroleum development. Such a tradition of wastefulness could hardly have been sustained without an overriding optimism. Continental abundance fostered the conceit that there would always be "more." Crucial to a developing American tendency to ignore harmful side-effects of resource exploitation, was the elaboration of this rustic optimism into a theory of externalities which emphasized only the beneficent spillover consequences of economic growth.

Frontier ideas emphasized progress by the vigorous, the venturesome, the vanguard of material exploitation—often without regard to long-run consequences.

Nature was seen as something different from and opposed to man. The leading academic exponent of laissez-faire individualism, William Graham Sumner of Yale, wrote in his 1896 essay, "Earth Hunger": "It is legitimate to think of Nature as a hard mistress against whom we are maintaining the struggle for existence." The consequential word was "against." The view behind the preposition was reflected in U.S. natural resource policy.

Facing a hard but plentiful land to the West, a society of hustlers on the make developed careless habits. Need wood? Chop a tree. Need coal? Dig a mine. Answers were uncomplicated by concern over harmful secondary effects. For instance: If felling a tree should kill some birds too, well, the forest would replenish its own in time.

Such a mentality readily fixed on individual material prosperity as the goal, and on the continent's material bounty as the means of its fulfillment. No end was seen of the one, for none was seen of the other. The myth of nature's cornucopia endured long after the disappearance of cheap land to the West. One historian has therefore suggested a more spacious concept of the frontier, referring not to a geographic boundary but simply to the "edge of the unused."

In his massive study *Law and Economic Change*, legal historian Willard Hurst stressed the principle underlying the frontier approach to the continent's first two great unused resources, arable land and harvestable trees:

The original forest was the work of centuries; its maintenance as a renewable resource required commitments counted by generations. Measured against the facts, the use men made of timber wealth was peculiarly revealing of their time preferences and the value they put upon pace and scale in economic growth.

In disposal of public timberlands, federal and state policy manifested the same pattern of preference for present over future yield as in disposition of public land . . .

The resulting pattern of forest denudation in Wisconsin, on which Hurst's case study focused, is illustrated in Fig. 1, which shows successive maps of the Craig Township, Wisconsin, woodlands over 120 years of exploitation.

As the edge of the unused continuously receded, Americans turned to a series of new resources. But always they followed the same exploitative pattern. Invariably too, they made full use of the legal and economic institutions developed to abet frontier practices—a subject to which we shall return in Chapter 10.

Thus frontiersmen harvested, but rarely replanted, whole forests. More profit-minded successors to the early woodcutter tradition got rich quick exploiting Appalachian coal fields. Then as coal veins played thin or industrial demand contracted, often they just as quickly got out. They left themselves and their customers—but not Appalachia—appreciably better off for the experience. Next came oil and gas. These were new resources, but they were taken in the old pattern. New petroleum reserves yielded to unplanned development. Early twentieth-century policies guaranteed every surface-landowner a share of the take, however wasteful. One scholar commented on the patchwork of individual ownership arrangements: ". . . diverse ownership of land in relatively small tracts and the rights attending ownership conspired to render rational production of oil a virtual impossibility." So intensive was drilling in early fields that the footing of one oil rig sometimes literally overlapped that of another. The rush to produce "black gold" depleted oil reserves.

Intensive development of each new resource never precluded extensive growth as well. The nation's history thus recorded consistent geographic expansion. In an underpopulated conti-

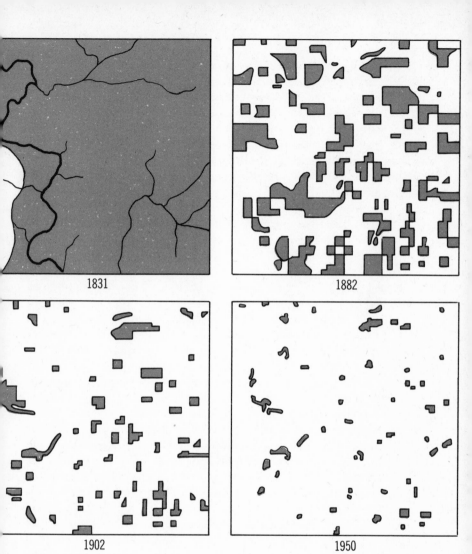

1831

1882

1902

1950

FIGURE 1

The Passing of the Forest

The woodlands of Cadiz Township, Green County, Wisconsin yielded to the 19th century expansion of population and agriculture. By 1950, only 3.6 percent of the original forested area remained in timber. (Adapted from John T. Curtis, "The Modification of Mid-Latitude Grasslands and Forests by Man," in William L. Thomas, ed., *Man's Role in Changing the Face of the Earth*, p. 726. Copyright © 1956 by The University of Chicago Press.)

nent, open space meant ready movement. The norm of self-reliance in a simple economy minimized neighborly involvement. Private initiative became the guarantor of material progress. Untrammelled individual pursuit of opportunity held the ticket to prosperity for all. What, then, should be the role of government in such a frontier culture, with its primitive sense of society and its idealization of material progress through private enterprise? Private practice on both the intensive and the extensive frontiers pointed to a specific pattern of public policy.

In due course, a laissez-faire, hands-off theory of government began to flourish. Nature's bounty seemed to necessitate little restraint of men's acquisitive urge. So it hardly seemed fit for government to step in as a regulator of interactions among men. On the contrary, the public role—to the extent that government got involved in the nation's economic life at all—evolved primarily as that of a stimulator of resource exploitation, not as a negative watchdog of the public interest.

Such a role was foreseen from the first. In his 1791 "Report to Congress on Manufactures," Secretary of the Treasury Alexander Hamilton urged active chaperonage by "the national councils" of Americans' entrepreneurial interests. Some thirty-four years later, President John Quincy Adams supported creation of a national university, patronage of new voyages of discovery, and erection of an astronomical observatory—in general, an expansive program of governmental scientific and economic stimulation, lest the nation "cast away the bounties of Providence" and condemn itself to "perpetual inferiority."

Laissez-faire enjoyed a late nineteenth- and early twentieth-century heyday. Yet even in the age of Social Darwinism, laissez-faire, American style, did not mean literal non-interference by government in private economy. It meant non-restraint of individuals but *active and persistent governmental efforts to stimulate national economic growth.*

From the time of the land grants and timber franchises onward, fostering private use of nature's abundance has been an abiding concern of U.S. law and policy. This concern remains evident in mineral subsidies and depletion allowances, in multifold river basin and hydro developments sponsored by Federal agencies, in Interior Department oil shale and coal gasification research, in active Atomic Energy Commission promotion of private peaceful uses of nuclear energy. Historian David Potter found the thread of historical continuity to lie in this "consistent endeavor of government to make the economic abundance of the nation accessible to the public." In America, resources passed on an historically unprecedented scale from public domain to private control—first the land and its increase under the generous nineteenth-century homestead laws and internal improvement programs; then valuable minerals, together with indefeasible rights to exploit them; and finally, the very air and water, to the extent that they are used as sinks to absorb wastes created in pursuit of private profit.

"Accenting the Positive": The Optimistic Theory of Externalities

Justifying government's role as an active sponsor of economic growth was an optimistic theory of the side-effects of enterprise.

Public largess was widely dispensed through such devices as subsidies and protective tariffs. Such subsidy practices could hardly exist as a dominant feature of America's economic landscape if the beneficent effect of positive externalities were not generally recognized. A whole policy framework has been erected on the foundation of this optimistic theory. A blind spot in American thought has persistently distracted attention from negative externalities, while emphasizing positive spillover effects of enterprise, such as "agglomeration effects" and external economies in industries with increasing returns to scale.

By this optimistic theory, subsidies are assumed to convey ultimate benefits to a much wider circle of recipients than those who immediately gain from a given preferential government program. Thus the Tennessee Valley Authority, though a regional development, was praised as having value to the nation as a whole. David Lilienthal, a director of the new agency, announced: "The first duty of the Tennessee Valley Authority in its power program is to set up what the President has called a 'yardstick' by which to measure the fairness of electric rates." With the TVA showing the way, everyone would ultimately gain from cheaper power.

Again, mineral depletion allowances of whatever level are justified on the ground that the entire society, not just coal and oil companies, gain from a healthy extractive industry.

Thus the recipients of public largess were not seen as mere profiteers from an industrial dole. Rather, it was recognized that every new, healthy private industry would produce spillover benefits for the economy as a whole. In this sense, what profited one would profit all. So all should favor government investment of public receipts on programs of economic stimulation, even when specific private interests seemed the immediate beneficiaries, for everyone would gain in the end.

Accordingly, even the hardiest free enterprisers have pressed for tariff protection, tax breaks, reduced mail rates—always on some variant of the theory that "what's good for them is good for America." In its elaborate framework of industrial subsidies, Americans have put their money where their mouths are in espousing the doctrine of positive externalities. And energy industries have stood right at the front of the line of those special interests willing to profit by this doctrine as recipients of public subsidies.

To the extent that they saw group benefits resulting from private pursuit of gain, exponents of the frontier economy did not ignore "externalities"—that is, effects of private action which do not enter the cost or gain calculations of those immediately involved as producers, buyers, or sellers. Economists discerned a coordinating mechanism—Adam Smith's "invisible hand"—whereby private transactions became harmonized into social benefit. The drive for profits would stimulate innovation and efficiency. All would share in the benefits, as free competition eliminated both over-priced and inferior-quality products. Herein lay much of laissez-faire's appeal. Beneficent externalities would emerge as by-products of individual selfishness working itself out in myriad decentralized market decisions.

Public intervention in the market seemed fully consistent with the prevailing economic doctrine, so long as it enriched the incentives for private selfishness rather than stifled acquisitiveness. The eighteenth-century aphorism "Private vice, Public virtue" became an intellectual system. In nineteenth-century America, it became public policy too.

The public virtues of industrial aggrandizement seemed especially conspicuous in the case of energy production. The apparent pertinence of the optimistic doctrine owed to certain technical and financial characteristics of the fuel industries. Specifically, energy-producing firms—from coal strip miners to electric utilities—require large capital investments even to get started. Since such investments must be paid for whether output is high or low, the large firm stands in a better position than the small one to face the considerable work involved in developing and exploiting sources of energy.

For example, it costs just about as much to drill a "dry hole" in speculative territory as it does to sink an oil well that turns out a gusher. (The price tag in either case is about $89 thousand, except if the well is off-shore, in which event the cost jumps to almost $560 thousand per well.) Again, the heavy equipment needed to shield a nuclear electric plant is of the same order of cost, whether the plant will serve a major city or a smaller load center. Small-scale operation saves relatively little in a capital-intensive industry. Conversely, high output adds little to costs—which are already largely sunk in fixed capital —but enables the investment to be spread over a larger revenue-yielding volume. So the unit costs of energy ostensibly go down as the scale of the operation goes up. That is why economists maintain that energy-processing firms are generally characterized by increasing returns to scale.

Gains in operating efficiencies from sophisticated equipment and techniques also permit lowered unit costs. The progressive firm's competitive position improves, and so does the whole industry's position vis-à-vis marketers of other fuel forms. So expansion again occurs. In turn, this leads to further economies of scale, again lowering unit costs. So energy industry unit costs constantly decrease with (1) the achievement of scale economies as a function of higher-volume output, and (2) technological improvements over time.

Lower unit cost means higher efficiency, reflected in improved economic returns within the expanding firm. But some of the benefit may be externalized. That is, it may spill over to other firms and even other industries, in which case, the benefit is known as an "external economy of scale."

For example, each energy firm's reach for scale adds to the pool of trained workers. It also adds to the store of technological know-how, and to the rate of improvement in related mechanical arts throughout society. Thus taken together, these firms turn out a by-product—socially useful facilities and skills —which could be supported only with difficulty by a few firms. This by-product, once it is available, makes further growth by still other firms just that much cheaper and easier. In this way, know-how gained in coal mining becomes an external economy for the uranium extraction industry—an externality that grows with the scale of each. The same pattern holds throughout the energy field.

Often firms both produce and benefit from external economies of scale as they profit from a particular geographic region's growing technological infrastructure. This process of unintended mutual stimulation illustrates what is known as the "agglomeration effect." As external economies help firms grow, they also attract new firms to the area. Such agglomeration helps explain the mushrooming of mercantile and industrial cities in a growing economy.

It has been this positive side of the externalties picture that the optimistic American economic doctrine has stressed. "Accentuate the positive"—to use the words from a popular song of the 1940's—seemed an appropriate injunction in terms of nineteenth-century theory. And this approach appeared equally consistent with the facts of an expanding economy. Moreover, the ubiquitous and unambiguous benefits of accelerating energy use seemed especially clear-cut. The continent revealed bountiful stocks of raw fuel. And the energy industry's economies of scale magnified positive externalities even as entrepreneurs expanded to increase their private profits.

Beyond Dollars and Cents:
Toward an Ecological Perspective

But what of the negative side of the picture? The frontier outlook tended to ignore—though it could not really eliminate— facts for which there was no room in the optimistic world-view.

Externalities can be negative as well as positive. In an economy driven by the profit motive, costs were cut, where possible, below the level needed to defray the real expenses of resource exploitation. *The free market pricing system failed to provide incentives to protect society's common property in fresh air, clean water, and undegraded land resources.*

Spillover costs are often diffuse in their effects. They are doubly difficult to recognize because they are rarely presented to the energy purchaser in dollars-and-cents terms. Often negative externalities take such non-pecuniary forms as air or water pollution.

In an ideal market—a phenomenon encountered only in the imagination of text writers—prices facilitate an optimum allocation of goods and services. (In such an ideal world, there are no "bads" because no consumer will pay a price for them. Hence no entrepreneur will produce them.) Every consumer is rational. Each consumer keeps diverting money from lesser to higher-benefit uses until he has an optimum mix of purchases. But the price mechanism succeeds as an optimal allocator of resources only if the consumer recognizes what costs he really has to pay in order to have more of one good than another. Hence there must be a close link between the market prices—the pecuniary prices—of physical goods and the benefits, burdens, and side effects which are actually entailed by the purchase of the goods. An externality is a failure in these conditions.

The market system presumes that the purchase price of fuel contains all the information needed by rational decisionmakers to regulate demand and determine supply. But consider the person whose health is impaired, or whose enjoyment of blue skies is prevented, by air pollution. Such an energy user cannot always convert his deprivations to dollar figures. With air pollution by smoke from fuel-burning, no market effectively evaluates the true effects of enterprise. Thus money passes from hand to hand. Goods and services pass too, but often with accompanying "bads"—as noxious fumes spread, after the purchased fuel is combusted—not confined to the payers or receivers of the dollars involved.

Such "bads" are true elements of energy costs, albeit in externalized form. They must therefore be considered in any full accounting of the environmental effects of fuel use. Accordingly, Chapters 2 and 3 set forth a framework for evaluating three major categories of non-pecuniary externalities: (1) "depletive waste," or the irrevocable using-up of resources due to inefficiency in fuel extraction and conversion; (2) "seral disturbance," or interference with any ecological cycles affronted by uncontrolled fuel use; and (3) "pollution," or the build-up of noxious wastes beyond the local environment's ability to assimilate residues. The "disvalue" of waste, of accelerated ecosystem aging, and of pollution is not fully measured in any market by pecuniary transactions among buyers and sellers.

Because damage is difficult, and perhaps impossible, to reckon in dollar terms, it is necessary to go beyond the market system in order to appraise the true costs of energy. As externalities cause the channels of money flow to diverge ever more widely from the channels of true costs and benefits, adequate appraisal of energy costs increasingly presupposes a shift away from strict reliance on traditional economic theory, with its confidence in pecuniary price as a measure of product costs. Robert Ayres and Allen Kneese have pointed out that economic theory still tends to ignore externalities as "exceptional cases" or "aberrations." In the eighth edition of Nobel laureate Paul Samuelson's *Economics*—the best-selling textbook in the history of higher education—the "external diseconomies" problem is explicitly treated in but 7 of 835 pages.

With some reason, then, Kneese and Ralph d'Arge argued in a presentation to Congress:

> . . . we see an urgent need to develop more relevant and operational economic models for dealing with pervasive externality phenomena. A few economists have observed that external diseconomies increase rapidly (nonlinearly) and pervasively with economic and population growth, but comparatively little has been done to formulate analytical or normative models based on this insight.

What appeared to classical theorists as "consumption" of goods was really mere conversion of marketable commodities, such as fuel, into unmarketable forms, such as ashes and spent heat. Having no useful commercial outlets, moreover, the products of conversion often just accumulate as pollutants. And what appeared to the frontiersman as an infinite resource base was depletable "energetic capital" invested by nature in wood and fossil fuels.

These traditional misperceptions suggest the need for a new perspective, an "ecological perspective." The ecological perspective avows a close relationship between man and the resources sustaining him. The ecological community nourishes man, but eventually calls in any debts incurred through unbalancing of the ecosystem's own cycles. Biologist Garrett Hardin has emphasized that attention to negative externalities necessitates a shift from the pecuniary to an ecological framework:

> The word "externality" is part of the word-magic of the business accountant. By this word-magic, the costs—to the firm, but not to society—are kept down, and business profits increased. To ecologists, the whole concept of externalities is fiction. All externalities are a true part of the cost.

In the individual's, as in society's and nature's, balance sheet—the external costs of energy must be counted because they really are costs. They do not *not* count because they are external.

Summary: True Cost versus Pecuniary Price

Frontier America's bounty fostered an exploitative culture based on private acquisitiveness. Material resources, when not disbursed through public giveaway programs, were to be allocated through a free market. The interests of private buyers and sellers were to be equilibrated through the price system.

The frontier culture accentuated the positive, believing in spillover benefits for all from continuing and concentrating enterprise. But the frontier ethic tended to minimize—though it could not in fact eliminate—the negative, in the form of harmful externalities. Hence American economic doctrine distracted attention from those adverse side-effects which threaten the validity of pecuniary pricing as a mechanism for resource allocation.

The allocation of the true values—the "goods" and the "bads" —associated with physical quantities exchanged depends on real costs, not on pecuniary prices. In the widening difference between true cost and pecuniary price lies much of the story of America's environmental despoliation. Indeed, in a growing economy, it is possible that adverse environmental effects of fuel use are already accumulating more rapidly than are the positive benefits of energy use. As true cost diverges from market price, misuse and waste—and the costs of American plenty—increase as well

REFERENCES

The energy growth statistics on p. 23 were taken from the 1969 *U.S. Statistical Abstract,* Department of Commerce, and from Claude Summers, "The Conversion of Energy," September 1971 *Scientific American.* See also:

1. Ali Bulent Cambel, *et al.*, *Energy R & D and National Progress* (Interdepartmental Energy Study, 1964);

2. *Considerations Affecting Steam Power Plant Site Selection,* 1968, by the Energy Policy Staff, OST, Executive Office of the President;

3. Hearings by the Joint Atomic Energy Committee, 91st Congress, published under the title, "Environmental Effects of Producing Electric Power" (1969).

The FDR anecdote and the David Potter quote are from Potter's *People of Plenty* (1954), pp. 80 and 123. The "edge of the unused" concept, by Dixon Ryan Fox, is developed on p. 145 of the Potter volume. The Hurst quote comes from the cited volume (1964), p. 112, and the opinion quoted at p. 26 comes from Erich Zimmermann, *Conservation in the Production of Petroleum* (1957), p. 93.

For historical perspective, see Hamilton's text in X Syrett 230 and the J. Q. Adams speech in II *Messages and Papers of the Presidents,* pp. 311–17. Richard Hofstadter's *Social Darwinism in American Thought* (1944) gives a full exposition of laissez-faire. For a more technical exposition of the economic theory applicable to market distribution of resources, see Robert Dorfman, *The Price System* (1964), especially Ch. 6; and Robert Heilbroner, *The Making of Economic Society* (1962), Ch. 3. The Samuelson text cited at p. 34 remains a standard for lucid presentation of what has become the conventional economics.

The well-drilling costs cited at p. 31 are taken from pp. 12–13 of Section I, *Joint Association Survey* (November 1970) by the American Petroleum Institute, the Independent Petroleum Association of America, and the Mid-Continent Oil and Gas Association.

The Lilienthal quote at p. 29 appeared in an April 25, 1934 TVA Press Release. The Kneese-D'Arge quote at p. 34 comes from a report by the Joint Committee on Economics, *Analysis and Evaluation of Public Expenditures: The PPB System* (91st, 1st, 1969), reprinted as Resources for the Future No. 80, "Pervasive External Costs and the Response of Society." The Ayres and Kneese comment on externalities appeared in the July 1969 *American Economic Review*. The statement by Garett Hardin is taken from his article in the May 10, 1969, *Saturday Review*.

An Early Oilfield: Signal Hill, California. The rush to exploit new-found reservoirs led to overdrilling, wasteful recovery, and accelerated depletion of the continent's finite petroleum reserves. (Shell Oil Company)

38

Consumption of the earth's stores of fossil fuels has
barely started; yet already we can see the end. In a
length of time which is extremely short when compared with the span of human history, and insignifi-
cant when compared with the length of time during
which man has inhabited the earth, fossil fuels will
have been discovered, utilized and completely consumed.

Harrison Brown,
The Challenge of Man's Future

2

Depletive Waste:
An Intergenerational
Externality

Pecuniary price measures the rate at which buyers can trade increments of one good for another in a market. But in nature's
energy conversions, such rates of exchange respond to the needs
of the ecological community, not to supply-demand balances in
some artificial market. In the basic physical processes which
produce man's fuel sources and determine the quality of his environment, nature's constants rather than variable market conditions control output.

The total output of fossil fuels available to man accumulated millennia ago. Sound husbandry of these fuels is essential, for unnecessarily inefficient conversion of coal, oil, and natural gas depletes the physical store irreversibly. The cost of such wastefulness is passed on to some future generation that will have either to work leaner deposits of raw fuels, or else to forego them altogether.

To gain a perspective on fuel wastage today, consider the energy-use patterns in the wood-based community that nurtured America's frontier ethic.

Fuel on the Frontier: The "Cheapness" of Energy

An ecosystem is a more or less self-sustaining community of organisms, plants as well as animals. A mature forest is such an ecosystem, self-regenerating through cycles of growth, decay, and regrowth. The forest depends on a continuing input of solar energy. This energy must be used in ways that insure replenishment. Each element of the community must contribute to the system as a whole, lest it upset the forest's balanced interactions among life cycles and food chains. If energy flows get seriously out of line, the forest dies.

Assume that a human being enters the forest, fells a tree, chops it, and hauls the wood off to burn for heat. What are the true costs to the ecosystem of this resource use, so typical of the frontiersman's primitive energy economy?

Assume that it takes six hours of hard work to prepare the firewood and, after burning, to clean the fireplace. In addition to a labor expense thus incurred—some 9.6 thousand British Thermal Units (henceforth, "Btu's) of work expended—the pioneer will have suffered soilage of his person and clothing. He will have exposed himself to accidental harm from a falling branch or a slip of the axehead. An area to store chopped wood by the hearth would have deprived him of alternative uses of that space—another cost. But even a full accounting of the pioneer's labor, plus such "extra" costs as soilage and hazard, gives a total *human* expenditure far smaller, in terms of energy expended, than the energy invested by *nature* to produce the raw fuel.

A typical firewood tree might yield one-fifth of a cord, perhaps 5.6 million Btu's. Such a tree grows by photosynthetic conversion of solar energy, with carbon dioxide and water, into living matter, or "biomass." But not all of nature's energetic investment—Btu's in the form of radiant energy from the sun—goes into growth. As shown in Fig. 2, less than one-tenth of 1% of solar energy hitting the earth gets used at all. Of the radia-

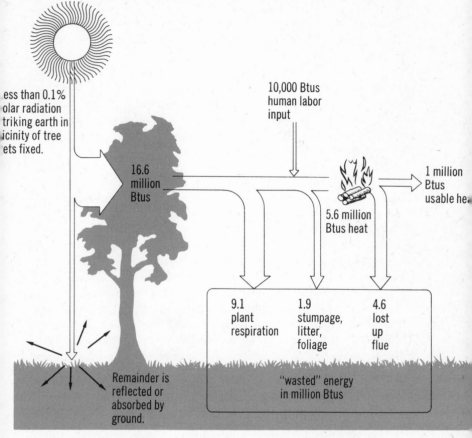

FIGURE 2

Energy Inputs and Outputs, Wood-Fuel Case

A relatively small input of work by the pioneer ostensibly yields a much larger return in space heat from burning wood. But this return represents a tiny fraction of the total energy invested when "nature's input" to grow the tree is taken into account. The apparent cheapness of energy depends on a frontier outlook which ignores nature's energetic costs of producing the raw fuel in the first place.

tion which is fixed by a growing plant, some 55% in temperate forests get "used up" in plant respiration. Moreover, a logger typically leaves 25% of a tree behind in foliage, chips, stump, and roots. So the Btu's which reach the pioneer's fireplace actually result from a more than 16.6 million Btu investment by nature.

Focusing only on the 10 thousand Btu or so human input suggests an extraordinary apparent ratio of benefits to costs. Even when the 5.6 million harvested heat yield is reduced to less than 1 million Btu's by adjusting for an estimated 85% wastage up the flue, the pioneer's energy still seems a fine bargain. But this illusion of cheapness results from the fact that the most important cost categories are externalized by the private decision-maker, even though they are internal to the ecological community—the forest.

In 1850 wood accounted for 92% of all energy from inanimate sources in the United States. The figure fell to 67% by 1875— when the pioneer model was still representative of some frontier areas—and below 30% only near the turn of the century. At high population densities, wood can answer society's thermal requirements only at the cost of the forest's own regenerative capacities. As more and more biomass then gets burned for heat fuel, less and less is available for replenishment.

Today the forests are largely gone. Flowing water at sites suitable for new hydro generation projects is not adequate to demand for electric power, which almost doubles each decade. Tidal forces defy harnessing, and solar energy is not economically competitive. With renewable energy income thus inadequate to the need, Americans dig into their principal: the stored energy in fossil fuels. Extraction of coal, oil, and gas couples the swampy forest ecosystems of more than 200 million years ago to today's high-demand society.

The nineteenth-century despoliation of America's forests, then, furnished a main impetus to the development of coal as an alternative fuel. But frontier traditions lingered—and so did the pioneers' optimistic tendency to ignore or understate externalities.

Measuring "Depletive Waste": Beyond Pecuniary Price

A sense of nature's bounty might have been suitable to the frontiersman's reliance on wood fuel, a self-regenerating energy form. But this sense distracted attention from the irreversibility of coal, oil, and gas consumption. Moreover, nature's energetic investment per unit of recoverable heat is even higher with the city-dweller's fossil fuels than with the pioneer's wood. About one hundred years of vegetative growth under proper climatological conditions—forests degenerating into oxygen-poor swamps, so accumulated biomass cannot rot away—will produce 4 feet of peat. This may ultimately turn into a 1 foot coal layer. Bituminous yield averages about 1.4 thousand tons per acre foot. So the 560 million tons of coal mined in 1969 represented the equivalent of a century's prehistoric primary ecological production over some 400 thousand acres—a once-only cashing-in of the dividends on past capital investments by nature.

Like the frontiersman's tree, each ton of coal represents an investment by nature in stored solar energy. But unlike the tree, a fossil fuel source cannot be replenished, except over geological time spans. With these fuels, man presides over the continuous dissipation of a fund of energy fixed in size by past biomass accumulation. Once dissipated, heat cannot be reharnessed. Hence real-world thermodynamic processes are said to be irreversible. They are one-way trips in the direction of time's arrow, yielding products like heat and ash, which can never be recombined in a sort of reverse combustion to call back the original fuel. Every ton of coal or barrel of oil burned becomes a bygone that is forever a bygone.

As indicated, the energetic costs to the overall physical system involved in producing fuel increase in the transition from wood to fossil fuels. Thus, increasing energetic costs of scale mark the shift from the frontiersman's autarkic community, capable of self-regeneration, to a high-demand urban civilization which spends thousands of years' prehistoric accumulation in decades. Nature's energetic balance-book extends over eons.

Man invested no resources to produce his raw fossil fuels. But this does not mean the resources were created cost-free. The "cost" was rather sustained by past ecosystems, in terms of energy stored through natural processes.

To the extent that depletion of nature's capital occurs inefficiently, it not only uses up resources but uses them wastefully. Untuned automobile engines spew uncombusted fuel to the atmosphere. Uninsulated homes waste heat. Older-vintage technology squanders energy because inefficient use of fuel still seems "cheaper" than upgrading of capital equipment. Such inefficiencies throughout contemporary energy exploitation processes give rise to a substantial loss of potentially useful energy. Because it draws down the natural resources available for conversion to energy, this loss may be termed "depletive waste."

It is easier to demonstrate the existence of depletive waste than it is to produce a scheme for accurate measurement of its magnitude. We know that miners unnecessarily waste coal, that petroleum workers waste oil. But *how* unnecessarily—and at what cost?

The capital investment by nature in fossil fuels cannot be completely represented by money in the economist's sense of all resources for which a given good can be incrementally traded off in the market. Indeed, there exists no evaluating market to coordinate nature's energetic exchanges across eons of time.

Nor is the irreversible character of energy use consistent with the underlying assumptions of pecuniary price. Charles Hitch and Roland McKean have stated the case for a money measure in benefit-cost analysis:

> Let us examine the justification for paying attention to monetary expense. What, in a fundamental sense, is the "cost" of a course of action? It is whatever must be given up in order to adopt that course. . . . Dollar costs do reflect what must be given up in order to adopt a particular policy. They reflect real sacrifices . . . because the prices of different items show the rates at which they can be substituted for each other.

The rates of substitution of one good for another, expressed in money terms, are thus assumed to work either way. But such reversibility is the exception in nature. Money can be "converted" into equipment for recovering raw energy, which in turn will be converted into heat and residues. Yet physically, this is a unidirectional process which, once completed, cannot be made to run in reverse.

The currency of the ecological community is *energy*. Like money, energy can be stored for future use. Also like money, it can be wasted—as some would say has been occurring all along in too rapid depletion of fossil fuels. But unlike money, energy is not readily subject to artificial creation or arbitrary manipulation. Needed are cost measures which, by getting closer to nature's own processes, become meaningful in nature's economy.

Disorganizing the Resource Base: The Extractive Phase

It would be possible to follow each fuel form from extraction to final conversion. The wastage sustained during the processing of each energy form—coal, oil, gas, nuclear and electric power—can then be roughly estimated in energetic terms. Such a cost-appraisal technique would begin to get beyond the pecuniary measure. It would ask not how many dollars a given inefficient practice costs but how many Btu's of nature's stored energy are irrevocably—and avoidably—used up over the entire fuel process in order to give off a single Btu of harnessable energy for man.

Coal. Coal reserves in the United States go to some 3.2 trillion tons, enough to power a highly industrialized society for generations, maybe even for centuries. But much coal is too deep, and some lies in veins too thin for profitable extraction. The energy is there potentially, but in such "disorganization"—small size of deposit, bad location—that only 50% of known reserves, about 42 million trillion Btu's, are foreseeably recoverable.

Further disorganization of the workable coal occurs during extraction. Such disorganization in effect wastes coal, passing on the costs of the resulting denial of useful energy to future generations.

In underground or "deep" mines, coal is often "gobbed out" of shafts, leaving vacant rooms behind, with the overburden of earth held up by pillars of unmined coal. When coal lies closer to the surface, it can be recovered by steamshovels which strip away or quarry whole seams. Or auger-drills can be used to dig out coal exposed along the side of a mountain.

Although extractive efficiency has steadily increased, all methods leave burnable coal underground. The bulk of coal pillars in deep mines can be reduced by substituting steel supports to prevent gobbed out shafts from caving in, but only at substantially increased coal production costs. Yet the room-and-pillar technique typically leaves half a coal seem in place. Strip and auger mining can physically waste upwards of 20% of coal in spoil or between the auger bore-holes. Thus extraction leaves some percentage of coal unrecovered—and probably forever unrecoverable, because once worked over it becomes prohibitively costly or too dangerous to go after. Hence the industry rule-of-thumb estimate: *As much coal gets wasted underground or in mine spoil as is delivered in consumable fuel.* The true cost per 260 therms of coal (the heat in a ton of bituminous) probably includes at least another 260 "wasted" in or around the mine.

This estimate ignores such other costs of resource disorganization as accidents during coal mining. Weakened rock strata and releases of volatile or poisonous gases are forms of environmental degradation in the workers' immediate locale. Injuries and deaths, as well as the persistent anxiety experienced with exposure to hazards by those who escape calamity, are alike due to an unstabilized extractive environment, occasioned by the mining activity itself.

Bureau of Mines analyses suggest a social loss of at least $9.5 thousand for every disabling injury in a coal mine. The social costs of each fatal accident run to about $8 thousand in the year of death plus almost one-third that figure annually for six to twelve years while survivors adjust to the loss of their breadwinner. An estimated 800 miners or ex-miners also die each year from black lung, contracted by breathing coal dust—another form of localized "resource disorganization." In 1968, the year of the Bureau of Mines study, the 15% of still living deep miners thought to suffer black lung generated social costs estimated at $21 million per working year, most of it from lost productivity, plus about $9.7 million in annual compensation payments. Subsequent federal legislation permitting higher benefits will probably cost at least $60 million annually in extra Social Security payments—thus displacing the cost of this "human waste" to the public sector.

Oil and Gas. During petroleum extraction, disorganization of the resource base occurs with less direct threat to oilfield worker safety than the parallel record for coal mining might suggest. Nevertheless, sheer physical waste during oil recovery may on occasion even exceed the 50% level of coal.

Oil occurs in minute voids in porous or permeable rock, not in free-flowing underground caverns. Viscous oil trapped at low pressures in dense rock may be locked in place, regardless of thermal potential or reservoir size. Dissolved natural gas reduces oil viscosity, helping it to flow toward a well. A gas cap, exerting pressure in the reservoir, often further assists as a lifting agent. Early oilmen, with neither a market for gas nor means to transport it if buyers were available, flared off their natural lifting agent. Reduced reservoir pressures then brought gas out of suspension in the oil, increasing viscosity and further inhibiting underground flow. Finally, pumping oil as quickly as possible compounded reservoir depletion, often leading to abandonment of the field before even a quarter of the oil had been recovered.

Oil take-rates today are, at least in theory, regulated to maximize long-run output. After stripping gas of liquid products, producers can recycle it into the reservoir to help hold pressures. Moreover, when primary recovery techniques fail, engineers may stimulate further output by waterflooding to give an artificial lifting agent. Ninety percent of the 548 thousand working oil wells in the United States were artificially stimulated at the end of 1969.

Yet even with advances in oil technology, recovery has not kept pace with new reservoir finds—and understandably so, since the industry tends to work from deeper, more difficult reservoirs as more easily tapped sources play out. Thus, of an estimated 556 million barrels discovered by petroleum exploration in 1969, only 120 million or 22% are thought to be ultimately recoverable. This figure contrasts with 25% recoverability of reserves found before 1920. Primary recovery ranges from about 30% of oil in place, when reliance is on viscosity-reduction by dissolved gas, to 35–45 percent when a gas cap gives extra lift. Secondary techniques—such as waterflooding or pumping stripped gas back into the reservoir for repressurization—can often halve these losses.

Gas is much more mobile or "fugacious" than is oil. Because of its low viscosity, it flows readily toward a well shaft sunk into a reservoir—and after extraction may be efficiently moved to market via a long-distance, high-pressure pipeline connected to the gas well. Hence wastage of gas, both below- and aboveground, is much lower than with coal or oil. Underground losses typically lie near 10%. But with gas too, economics sometimes dictates earlier abandonment rather than continued operation at low pressure or against reservoir impermeability.

Nuclear Fuel. As with coal and petroleum, the crucial consideration for commercial exploitation of uranium is the concentration of ultimately fissionable material in accessible areas. Hence a mine will be worked only if its gross yield promises a dollar profit higher than the opportunity costs of the project. But in extraction and milling, perhaps 10–15 percent of the energy content will be lost, dispersed in spoil, tailings, and underground waste, making later recovery much more difficult and hence much more expensive.

By 1980 nuclear fuel may generate up to one-third of the nation's electricity, about 1 trillion Kwh. Based on these projections, the Atomic Energy Commission has estimated an annual need for 38 thousand tons of uranium oxide by 1980, or more than three times current levels. Cumulative use of 237 thousand tons by 1980 will exceed known reserves of about 161 thousand tons. New discoveries are counted on to satisfy the need. Yet unless a breeder reactor is developed by the 1980's, a uranium shortage could develop.

Regardless of fuel form, it is inefficiency—in extraction, in transportation, in conversion—which multiplies the drain on resources occasioned by a given output of useful heat. Fortunately, efficiency in energy use has shown an ascending profile. Modern mining equipment has raised productivity while lowering underground losses. Average thermal efficiencies of heat machines increased—or alternatively, waste output per unit of heat decreased—by almost one-third between 1940 and 1960. "Unitized" coal trains that haul only fuel from mines to markets in huge loads, covered bunker cars, and experimental slurry pipelines reduce waste from coal spillage in the transportation phase. Fracturing of dense rock with underground atomic explosions promises to make previously unrecoverable natural gas workable. Putatively spent petroleum reservoirs are regularly bought up and subjected to new secondary recovery techniques. Advanced waterflooding technology, for example, can sometimes bring 90% of a reservoir's store to the surface.

The middle column in Table 1 shows the potential energy rendered practically unrecoverable as a result of extracting 260 therms of coal, oil, gas, or uranium with current technology. But suppose that technology increases efficiency in resource recovery 50% by the time that a given future generation faces depletion of the fuel in question. The third column then shows the energy which *would have been* available to that future generation if the resource disorganization had not occurred in the first place.

TABLE 1

Hypothetical Cost of a Therm of Fuel to a Future Generation

	Therms Recovered	Energetic Cost	Fuel Denied
Coal	260	260	130
Oil	260	100	50
Gas	260	30	15
Uranium	260	34	17

It is not possible to estimate the dollar value of fuel denied some future generation by extractive inefficiencies. First, the estimate itself presumes knowledge of the rate of technical advance, since this rate determines what percentage of the energetic cost will actually represent "Fuel Denied" to a given future generation. Second, no satisfactory monetary discount rate is available to fix an accurate present value on events likely to occur so far—say, more than fifty or even one hundred years —into the future.

What *can* be said is that the energetic costs of inefficient fuel extraction are considerable. The depletive waste phenomenon merits not only recognition but study with an eye to reduction, in the energy accounts of a society whose traditional prodigality already portends a rendezvous with scarcity in several fuel categories.

The "Heat Costs of Heat": Energy Conversion

More than 34 million families heat with gas. Coal has declined as a source of residential energy, but oil and electricity heat a significant percentage of the nation's homes. Between 1970 and 1980, a three-fold increase in electrically heated households—up to 11.3 million—has been predicted. Commerce Department estimates in the 1970 *U.S. Statistical Abstract* indicate that more than one-fifth of the nation's households also have air conditioning, which uses thermodynamic transfers for space cooling of interiors—but at the cost of increased vented heat to the buildings' exteriors. Overall, space heating is thought to account for 10% of per capita energy use in the United States.

How efficiently is that heating-cooling market being supplied?

A 1970 study by the Organization for Economic Cooperation and Development reported that 21% fuel savings could be achieved if new dwellings in Western Europe were to receive optimum insulation. Adjusting for improved insulation in older buildings too, a weighted average fuel saving of 14% per year would result from an effective OECD-area heat-saving program. This figure suggests major heat losses in the United States due to faulty insulation—at least 20 billion therms annually if 10% of natural gas converted and 34% of oil is assumed to go into space heating.

Conversion of fuel for space heating puts a premium on maximum warming value *after* combustion. But the efficiency of the conversion process itself becomes important when fuel is used to produce work. The object then is to translate the maximum fraction of the fuel's energetic potential into the organized motion of machines. This objective dominates more than half the overall energy market. Transportation alone accounts for 25% of total energy demand, and industrial-commercial uses for another 39%.

Of the energy in each unit of fuel, combustion converts only a fraction into a force that pushes a piston or, through the medium of expanding steam, drives a turbine. The maximum theoretically achievable efficiency in fuel conversion depends on the difference between the temperatures of combustion and of the machine's exhaust. Perfect efficiency—no waste—would require an exhaust temperature of absolute zero. This is impossible. So even a machine that is perfectly designed, constructed, tuned, fueled, and exhausted wastes some energy.

Within the theoretical limit, further losses occur because actual construction and operation never realize the design optimum. For example, the actually achievable 40% efficiency of the best new steam electric power plants is to be compared with the 60% theoretically achievable maximum in the largest units. Operating efficiencies are even lower in other machines, e.g., automobiles with 10% at typical driving profiles.

Because of these cumulative heat losses due to inefficiency, *every therm leaving conversion in mechanically harnessable form implies an additional energy loss at least half again as large. By almost any reckoning, this loss at 1970's use levels would exceed 250 billion therms annually.* Whatever portion of this total might be saved by feasible gains in efficiency, or readily reserved for later use with more efficient technology, may be entered as depletive waste on the debit side of society's energy ledger.

Electric Power: The True Premium Fuel

Conversion inefficiencies which compound depletive waste sustained as a result of extractive inefficiencies, are themselves compounded when the primary fuel is burned to produce electricity. The inefficiencies of the added stages in the process of electrical generation themselves become additive. Further losses in transmitting and distributing the power make this clean, convenient energy form our true "premium fuel" on the cost as well as on the benefit side of the equation.

In 1970, some 76% of all fossil fuel was "converted" only once —to give space heat, or to move a car, or to turn industrial machinery. The remaining fuel was converted into electricity, then distributed. In most cases the energy was ultimately reconverted into mechanical form—into the motion of electrically powered machines, ranging from commuter railroad engines to home hair dryers. By following electric power backwards, from ultimate use to ultimate source, the cumulative depletive pressures of this energy form on fossil and nuclear fuel resources can be gauged.

The power lines used to transmit and distribute electricity for consumption are perhaps the most permeable, "leaky" components of the energy order. Line losses are on the order of 3 thousand watts out of every 26 thousand introduced to a 1 mile stretch of 23 hundred volt transmission line. A comparable 10% line loss occurs in local distribution.

Thus for coal-generated power—which included 65% of all electricity in the early 1970's—energy losses per ton of primary fuel include 260 million Btu's left underground, plus 164 million wasted to the environment as "unharvestable" heat at 37% plant efficiency during conversion, plus another 10 million dissipated by line resistance before the energy has traveled to the consumer. Typical electric appliances have 75% efficiency. Thus another 21 million Btu's will be lost for the 86 million actually delivered to the consumer. Such losses—455 million Btu's for every 65 million converted to useful work—must be read into the energy accounts of a society which will present well over 25% of its energy in 1980 to the ultimate consumer in the form of electric power. Thus *growing demand for electricity stimulates a disproportionately rapid depletion of fossil and nuclear reserves to make up in higher levels of generation what electricity's segment of the energy order loses in transit and conversion.*

To anticipate the resource implications of this depletive pressure for the near future, Table 2 breaks out, for the projected 1980 energy demand in the United States, the allocation of Btu's actually used in power generation (the first subcolumn under each major primary category) and for space heat or direct conversion of fuel into work (shown combined as "H & W").

Each line in Table 2 shows the total number of Btu's that must be input at that stage to yield the number of Btu's, after losses to inefficiency, shown on the next line. In 1980 some 100 Btu's of energy out of every 400 ultimately demanded by customers will come from electric power. At the supply end, each such illustrative increment of 400 Btu's will come from a mix of five primary fuels—the fossil fuels, plus nuclear and hydro, in a 360:40 ratio. Each form (except maybe hydro) will occasion

TABLE 2

Depletive Waste in BTU's
(Projected in 1980)[a]

| | Fossil Fuels | | Nuclear | Hydro | Total | |
	Power	H & W	All Elec.	Power	Power	H & W
In Ground	362	1,146	193	—	555	1,146
1. After Extraction [b]	200	707	135	27	362	707
2. After Conversion to Electricity [c]	87	—	48	13	148	—
3. After Line Losses	80	—	44	12	136	—
4. Useful Power Final Conversion [d]	60	300	33	7	100	300

[a] Percentages of fuels in 1980 energy market and by sector based on Figs. 1–8, Bureau of Mines Information Circular No. 8384.
[b] Assumes 60% recovery of oil, 90% of gas, 50% mechanical efficiency in hydro turbines.
[c] Fossil fuels at 40% efficiency, nuclear at 35%.
[d] Using 50% efficiency for coal and gas, 40% for oil to reflect lower efficiency of automobiles.

some depletive wasting of potentially useful energy in disorganization of the resource base (line 1) and losses in ultimate conversion (line 4). About 78% of coal, 20% of gas, 2% of oil, and virtually all nuclear fuel is expected to be converted to electricity. Therefore, added waste is occasioned by those fuels' intermediate conversions (line 2) and deliveries (line 3) in the form of electrical power.

Thus, 100 Btu's of usable electric power require disturbance of the equivalent of 555 Btu's of potential energy in the ground. The difference is energy lost—for the most part, irretrievably lost—between discovery and use. By contrast, 100 Btu's used in

space heating or as a direct motive force necessitates the disturbance of only about 382 Btu's in the ground. In effect, a 173 Btu
energetic "surcharge" is exacted for every 100 Btu's of electric
power as compared with direct use of the fossil fuels. Fig. 3 illustrates the losses to various forms of inefficiency which occur
to produce 100 usable Btu's of electric power and 300 in non-
electric energy.

The Costs of Waste:
In the Market, in Nature, in Society

Some waste is inevitable. Irreversible heat processes always increase the disorderliness of matter, degrading energy and decreasing the resource's usability. This fact of nature can be
stayed by no wishful thinking. Other forms of physical waste are
avoidable, but only at prohibitive costs. Thus coal, oil, and uranium left underground as *physical* waste may be an inescapable
economic cost of extracting fuel. Yet part of the waste encountered in all phases of energy use must be charged to avoidable
inefficiencies in a system that ignores the claims of future generations for resource conservation.

An individual, with his relatively short lifespan, is concerned
with near-term gains and costs. But society as a corporate body
is intended to outlive all the individuals composing it. Hence
society must regard interests far into the future.

Pecuniary price can indicate relative gains and costs in a contemporary market. But markets less reliably serve the interests
of generations unborn. In theory, unused resources have a present value which is set in the market by the "discount rate."
This rate reflects how quickly the good loses value as its use is
anticipated to be deferred. A low discount rate, therefore, means
that relatively little value is thought to be lost if the resource in
question is not used up now but saved for the future. In principle, reflecting the socially optimal discount rate in current fuel
prices would permit market decisions leading to a rate of depletion which maximizes the value of the resource over time.

But in practice, there are obvious dangers in long-term fore-
casting of values for goods in a context of rapid technological

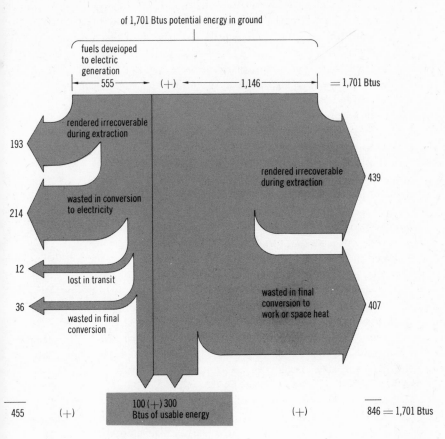

FIGURE 3

Depletive Waste of Fuels in Btu's

In 1980, more than 1,700 Btu's of potential energy in a raw state will have to be exploited in order to produce 400 Btu's of usable energy, assuming electric and non-electric end uses in a 1:3 ratio. Some 1,301 Btu's worth of fuel are lost as waste or are rendered virtually unrecoverable in raw form, with electric power accounting for a disproportionately high percentage of this "energetic cost."

change. Moreover, even if the theoretical feasibility of setting a socially optimum discount rate were conceded by all economists, in such a present-oriented society as the United States, the technique might still be applied without due regard for future generations' interests. Thus because of difficulties in application of the discount rate principle, the market is suspect as an allocator of resources in the intergenerational time frame. Again, there is need to supplement economic theory with an ecological perspective.

Specifically, "nature's investment" in creating the raw fuel must be considered by energy policymakers, even though the energetic costs of producing a resource are irrelevant to market pricing. Fossil fuels are presented to man as the products of completed physical processes. They are virtually "free goods," ready-made by nature.

The wood that a manufacturer turns into a chair, or the iron ore from which a foundryman makes a beam, may also be viewed as a free good to be harvested by man. Yet human fabrication plays a much larger relative role in producing the chair and the beam. With these items, man and nature "cooperate," making more nearly equal energetic investments, to fashion a useful artifact. With fossil fuels, nature's contribution is clearly primary. Man need only extract and refine before final use. Furthermore, of course, the wood may be recycled into other products, as the steel beam may be melted down and reshaped. But a fossil fuel, once used, is gone forever.

Since the solar energy input which is stored in the fossil fuels is not offered to man on a *quid pro quo* basis, nature's investment never draws resources from other uses which are pecuniarily evaluated by buyers and sellers. Therefore the original energy input is not evaluated in the market. Nor does it necessarily enter into the price an individual must pay for fuel.

On the other hand, as a fossil fuel gets scarcer, its current price in the market gets higher. Less valued uses—or maybe more valued uses of the resource by poorer people—are unable to compete for the dwindling stocks. Eventually, all uses by rich and poor alike will disappear, unless the fuel can somehow be renewed at a cheap enough price to buoy demand. This might require artificial recycling of the biogeochemical systems which originally gave rise to the fuel—that is, duplicating nature's handiwork by industrial synthesis. Dissipated heat cannot be recycled. But the complex organic molecules of fossil fuels can be. And one day they may have to be. Nature's ecological investment suggests the magnitude of energy and materials required for such synthesis. So reduction of depletive waste does not so much save the fuel itself, as it saves the possible later costs of synthetic recombination of elements.

The thermodynamic investment needed to produce a fossil fuel is absorbed by nature only once. The raw good is free (relatively) to man only the first time he uses it. It takes about fifteen times as much energy to synthesize a hydrocarbon molecule as is converted into usable heat when the molecule is oxidized. Therefore, it is unlikely that hydrocarbons will ever be synthesized for heat.

But a society committed to high living standards is just as unlikely to outgrow its need for, say, certain chemical resources now abundant in the fossil fuels. Petrochemical feedstocks are already the "highest value" uses of petroleum, and this market will furnish petroleum's fastest growing demand. Every therm used for space heating or electric power generation today detracts from some future generation's natural endowment of such feedstocks, which are ecologically costly to produce, however apparently "cheap" these fuels are in dollar terms.

Summary: The Costs of Waste

The main barrier to recovery of coal, petroleum, or uranium from leaned-out sources is *economic undesirability*. Old mines or reservoirs may just not be worth reopening, so the energetic costs of extraction are simply absorbed and the use of untappable resources forever forgone. But the obstacle to future use of heat wasted during fuel conversion is sheer *physical impossibility*. Thermodynamic processes yield unrecycleable products like heat and ash.

Again, to some degree the unrecallability of fuel depletion must be considered a fair cost of enjoying the energy at all. But to some degree also, avoidable inefficiencies in the extraction and transmission of energy, as well as in conversion, reduce the physical stock of fuels likely to be in the future exploitable. Thus depletive waste occurs as a consequence of energy use at any level of technology. Moreover, growing demand for electrical power compounds physical wastage of primary fuels per unit of useful output, multiplying depletive waste. Although these categories of waste do not yield to pecuniary appraisal, the energetic costs run to millions of billions of Btu's every year. These costs represent a substantial past investment by nature to produce the fossil fuels. Though this investment may be irrelevant in the buyer-seller market, it is of high consequence for the long-term interests—and cost-accounts—of society.

REFERENCES

The chapter epigraph comes from p. 168 of Brown's book (1954).

The figures used in the pioneer example come mostly from Edward Kormondy, *Concepts of Ecology* (1969), pp. 14–27, 153 —with supplementary help from staff members of Hartley Tree Service Company, Princeton, New Jersey, on the technicalities of tree harvesting and cording. Statistics on U.S. energy sources, expressed as percentages at p. 42, are taken from Earl Cook, "The Flow of Energy in an Industrial Society," September 1971 *Scientific American*. Coal yield is estimated in the Interior Department's *Surface Mining and Our Environment* (1967), p. 114.

The quote at p. 44 comes from p. 26 of the Hitch-McKean book which introduced the vogue of benefit-cost analysis, *The Economics of Defense in the Nuclear Age* (1960).

Estimates of the costs of coal mining accidents and disease are taken from two internal Bureau of Mines staff studies: Lucille M. Langlois, "Coal Workers' Pneumoconiosis: A Comparative Cost Analysis," 1968 Draft Information Circular, esp. pp. 22–24; and David B. Brooks, "The Cost of Coal Mine Accidents" (July 17, 1969) —both made available through the then Director of the Bureau, Mr. John F. O'Leary. The compensation estimates at p. 47 are taken from the May 20, 1971, *New York Times*. See also Duane Lockard, *The Perverted Priorities of American Politics* (1971), Ch. 1.

Petroleum recovery statistics come from the February 18, 1970 *World Oil* and from 24 *Reserve Data* (December 31, 1970) by the American Gas Association, American Petroleum Institute, and Canadian Petroleum Association. See also Richard Hughes, *Oil Property Valuation* (1967), Ch. 10.

Figures relating to gas and electrically heated households are from the Edison Electric Institute and the Interior Department's 1969 *Minerals Yearbook.* The estimates of fuel use for heating appear in an Alvin Weinberg article in the July–August 1970 *American Scientist;* see esp. p. 413. Weinberg is Director, Oak Ridge National Laboratory, site of a continuing energy study.

Electric power consumption statistics at p. 52 come from unpublished research as part of the Oak Ridge study by Oran L. Culberson. Also useful on electric power demand and supply are FPC's *National Power Survey,* both the 1964 study and portions of the 1971 update; Edison Electric Institute, *Electric Utility Industry Statistics;* and *Electric Power and the Environment,* by the Energy Policy Staff, OST (August 1970). Mr. William Webb, Director of FPC's Information Office, provided copies of pertinent statistical publications in this field, such as FPC-R-75, *Typical Electric Bills* (1969), and *Steam Electric Plant Construction Costs* for current years. On electric power's environmental impact, see also:

1. L. O. Barthold and H. G. Pfeiffer, "High Voltage Power Transmission," May, 1964 *Scientific American;*

2. Citizens' Advisory Committee on Recreation and Natural Beauty, Laurence Rockefeller, Chairman, *The Electric Utility Industry and the Environment* (November 1966),

3. Working Committee on Utilities, *Report to the Vice-President and to the President's Council on Recreation and Natural Beauty* (December 27, 1968).

The "insulation loss" estimates at p. 50 are in OECD Draft A/ DAS/CSI.476, and the apportionment of gas and oil to the heating market is based on the Bureau of Mines March 23, 1971, *Mineral Industry Survey* report.

Warren E. Morrison and Charles L. Readling, *An Energy Model for the United States,* Bureau of Mines Information Circular 8384, presents the projections underlying Table 2. These data were supplemented with figures on the current energy market in "Outlook for Energy in the United States" (1968), a Chase Manhattan Bank report.

Economy versus Ecosystem: The Chesapeake Bay. As a result of heavy use of industrial coal without adequate effluent control, Chesapeake Bay water and the local air shed serve as "environmental sinks" for energy wastes. (Grant Heilman Photography)

The balance of nature is not the same today as in Pleistocene times, but it is still there: a complex, precise, and highly integrated system of relationships between living things. . . . Man, too, is part of this balance. Sometimes the balance is in his favor; sometimes—and all too often through his own activities—it is shifted to his disadvantage.
Rachel Carson,
Silent Spring

3

Energy and Ecology

~~~~~~~~~~~~~~~~~~~~~~~~~~~~~~~~

Reckoning the externalized cost of depletive waste in energetic terms underscores the fact that patterns of energy flow—even over millions of years, and even under extreme human interference with nature's pace of change—follow definite physical laws. A consideration of these ecological and thermodynamic laws will introduce an analysis of energy costs under two remaining categories of environmental externality: "seral disturbance" and "pollutive build-up."

Nature was storing value (e.g., saving thermal energy in fossil fuels) and exchanging goods (e.g., converting solar energy into vegetation) long before man used money for similar functions. And nature's consequential benefit-cost ratio, reckoned in energetic currency, is the long-run balance between energy photosynthetically converted into new biomass (on which all other life depends), and energy used in respiratory activities, including growth, reproduction, and combustion or degradation of food and fuel.

Perfect balance between production and consumption of energy is rarely achieved in a single ecological cycle. That is, respiration hardly ever "uses up" the exact energetic input to a given organ or organism. As a result, residues are produced. These residues require, for their ultimate assimilation, a network of transport media to carry effluents away to adequate ecological sinks. Such transport media couple productive ecosystems (which yield a net output of consumable matter, whether in the form of sewage, waste products or fossil fuels) to ecosystems capable of assimilating, breaking down, or dispersing the vented substances. The proper starting point for an ecologically responsible energy policy lies in attention to the system of artificially and naturally coupled "producing" and "consuming" ecosystems.

Production-Consumption Balance and Ecosystem Coupling

Metropolitan areas originate most of the demand for food and fuel. These densely populated urban centers are characterized by high ratios of consumption to production. Since a population in New York, Chicago, or Los Angeles eats more than it can itself supply, it requires that most of its food energy be produced elsewhere. This requirement ties the city to the agricultural hinterland which produces the population's food, thus balancing the production-consumption ledger. The energy economy follows the same pattern. Some areas (e.g., coal- and oil-producing states) are sources of the fuel which people elsewhere—mostly in cities—convert to heat. Artificial links such as railroads, pipelines and tankers, and electric powerlines connect the energy-producing with the consuming sectors.

In nature, transport media may sometimes serve as sinks for effluents, and vice versa. The natural network of coupling and assimilative agents includes the atmosphere and hydrosphere, which are commonly used to carry off effluents like smoke or waste heat; the lithosphere, or band of rock and soil about the earth; and the biosphere—the film of living organisms with an important role as a physical assimilant of certain gaseous and solid effluents. Thus, air pollutants may get trapped in a person's lungs, which become a sink for the vented particulates. Given adequate coupling, whether by natural or artificial means, excess wastes from one ecosystem can be carried to other systems capable of assimilating them. Otherwise they tend to pile up locally, causing pollution.

With adequate coupling too, a related set of ecosystems will tend toward a balance between output and consumption. Thus, nature's respiratory processes must ultimately assimilate the organic matter which results from the biological processes of production. In the same way, a balance between output and consumption of goods must ultimately obtain in the economy. The reason for this general tendency toward an equilibrium, at both the ecological and the economic levels of analysis, is basically chemical. Most outputs of productive or constitutive processes are themselves energetically charged. Hence they are subject to further reaction, which is normally degradative or destructive in its effects. Such reaction will occur if the materials are transported to an area which provides conditions conducive to further chemical change.

Repeated experimentation has confirmed the basic physical principle known as the Second Law of Thermodynamics, that energy-rich compounds tend to decay to lower-energy compounds, accompanied by the release of heat. This assimilative-degradative process may be speeded artificially (as by burning fuel in a furnace), or through absorption in the ecosystem (as by biological decomposition of vented unspent fuel). If catalysts cannot be supplied, or in the absence of suitable ambient conditions for the reaction to go forward quickly, the degradation will occur geochemically, over a longer period. However accomplished, *what gets composed eventually gets decomposed,* with constitutive and destructive processes netting out over a whole network of coupled ecosystems, and often over substantial time spans.

Representative production-consumption ratios for some common kinds of ecosystems are shown in Fig. 4. Systems beneath the diagonal consume more than they produce. They feed on free energy obtained from detritus "imported" from other sources. Such failing systems are exemplified by polluted waters suffering rapid depletion of available oxygen. These net consum-

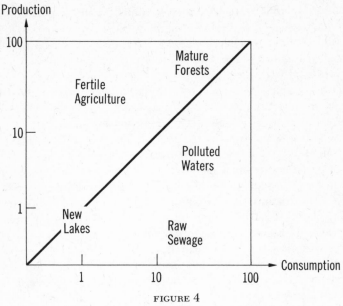

FIGURE 4

Typical Ecosystem Production / Consumption Values
(Tons / Acres / Year)

A fertile field in cultivation yields a marked excess of biomass output. Much of this excess of energetically charged matter eventually finds its way across the diagonal to a "net consuming" ecosystem where, in the form of garbage or sewage, it is decomposed. (Adapted from E. P. Odum, *Fundamentals of Ecology*, 3d ed., W. B. Saunders Company, 1971.)

ing systems are ultimately coupled to ecological sectors above the diagonal. The latter sectors produce the excess which overloads the system in question. They produce, for example, crops and fuel that in time become oxygen-eating sewage and industrial wastes. In this case, city sewers and factory drainpipes furnish the coupling agents.

The matching of production to consumption, of composition to decomposition, most often occurs over a network of linked ecosystems, rather than within a single system. Linkages among ecosystems are needed because a given productive region can rarely serve simultaneously as a sink. Thus a high-yield ecosystem, whether it produces coal or crops, normally "pays for" its productive ability by a diminished capacity to consume. A coal mine cannot be backfilled while it is being worked—cannot simultaneously produce energy and store the wastes created by the extractive process. Nor will a farm field long flourish if its crops are buried under rubbish and garbage.

Thus in proportion as a mine or a farm is productive, it creates a requirement for more rather than less acreage *elsewhere* to absorb the residues it ultimately creates.

Consider a concrete, familiar example—that of the interacting ecological cycles which increasingly contribute to agriculture-associated pollution. Today an elaborate transportation network ties America's high-yield croplands to major consuming ecosystems in the cities. But before the elaboration of this coupling network, rural America was a patchwork of farms. Each farm was a more or less separate little ecosystem in which a high percentage of organic matter got cycled internally. As Fig. 5 suggests, such a farm approximated—admittedly, very roughly— the ideal model of a "closed" system, with minimum exchanges beyond its own boundaries. Plants drew nutrients from the soil. Perhaps the farmer sold off part of his harvest. If so, some stored energy, plus nutrients from the soil incorporated in crops, did leave the locale. But he kept the rest in silage for his animals. The animals ate and excreted, and thus returned nutrients to the soil as manure. Aided by some occasional imports of purchased fertilizer, the cycle could turn over and over.

Agricultural modernization brought multiplied yields. Today each acre can feed many more persons than was once the case, and these persons live much farther from the food source. With growing affluence, consumers demand more and more expensive fare—expensive both pecuniarily and ecologically. Thus consumer tastes increasingly demand that beef be substituted for lower-protein foods.

Efficient cattle husbandry requires that the animals be readied for slaughter in feedlots, rather than being permitted to graze open ranges freely. It is cheaper to harvest grain by machine and transport it to concentrations of immobile cattle. Letting the animals themselves "work for" their meals slows their weight-gains and toughens the flesh. In the two hundred feedlots in the state of Kansas alone, some 5.5 million cattle and 1.3 million

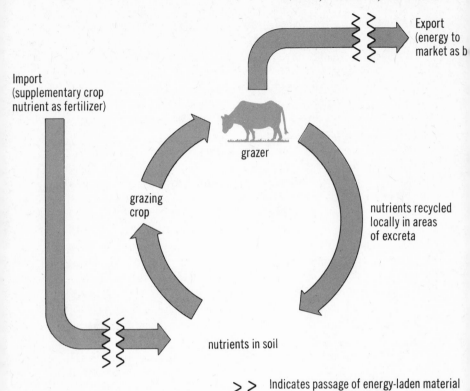

Import
(supplementary crop
nutrient as fertilizer)

Export
(energy to
market as b

grazer

grazing
crop

nutrients recycled
locally in areas
of excreta

nutrients in soil

Indicates passage of energy-laden material
across boundary of local ecosystem **via** some
coupling mechanism (**i.e.** truck brings in
fertilizer, rail cars take out beef on hoof).

FIGURE 5

Nutrient Cycle in Traditional Cattle Grazing

hogs excrete the sewage equivalent of 70 million people. The
nutrients in this effluent, of course, come from the fodder that
has been carried to the animals. These nutrients are removed
forever from the croplands which manure from grazing cattle
used to replenish. At the same time, the concentration of effluent
renders the wastes unassimilable by the local ecosystem. So the
excreta run off the land, seeking a sink elsewhere. The wastes
end up in rivers and streams, where decay prevents drinking
and even swimming throughout Kansas.

Thus increased production of an energetically charged substance creates a need for increased consumptive capacity elsewhere, and unforeseen problems can result for that "elsewhere" if the assimilative capacity is insufficient. Conversely, heightened demand at the consumer end usually requires some adjustment in production. Thus, since feedlot cattle husbandry removes nutrients from the soil and eventually concentrates them as pollutants in a few locales, farmers must replenish their lands with fertilizer imported from outside the ecosystem. Fig. 6 on the next page illustrates the resulting pattern.

In the quarter-century following World War II, inorganic nitrogen fertilizer use increased about seven-fold. From 15–35 percent of this nitrogen eventually washes off into local waters. In the mid-1960's, agricultural runoff added almost seven times the tonnage of pollutive nitrogen to United States waters, as did all municipal sewage. The ecological imbalance already created by depletion of soil nutrients through transport of crops from the locale is compounded. The farm's soil is unable to assimilate and hold all the fertilizer added to it. Therefore it yields a pollutive quantity of the added nitrogen to neighboring aquatic systems, which begin to function as an ecological sink.

The Ecosystem-Economy Interface

As the effluent burden grows, more and more systems are linked into the network of productive and consuming sectors by which nature strains to restore ecological balance. The same pattern holds true when the energetically charged matter is fuel rather than food.

Wastes left by incomplete consumption or uncontrolled venting of the products of coal mines, oil rigs, and gas wells must also find ultimate sinks. Failure to take up or "consume" these wastes in a controlled manner will threaten ecological imbalance while nature strains to readjust the network of linked ecosystems that are affected. Long-term environmental degradation —as in the polluted waters of Kansas—may result once new natural sinks to consume the effluents have been brought into play.

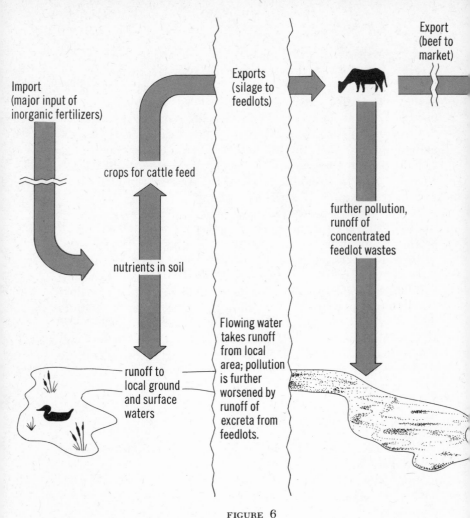

Import
(major input of
inorganic fertilizers)

Exports
(silage to
feedlots)

Export
(beef to
market)

crops for cattle feed

further pollution,
runoff of
concentrated
feedlot wastes

nutrients in soil

Flowing water
takes runoff
from local
area; pollution
is further
worsened by
runoff of
excreta from
feedlots.

runoff to
local ground
and surface
waters

FIGURE 6

Water Pollution by Inorganic Fertilizers
and Feedlot Runoff

Modern agriculture needs an extensive network of ecosystems. Heavy imports of fertilizers to croplands are followed by export of grains to cattle feedlots, and then of cattle to market. Often, both fertilizers and manures are also "exported" from their points of use or origin, fouling entire water systems.

"Consumption" actually is a misnomer when applied to the physical processes of energy conversion. Combustion changes a fuel's form, but does not literally use it up. In fact, residues from combustion exceed the weight of intake fuels because the coal or petroleum molecules are combined with oxygen during conversion. Thus the hallmark of a so-called high-consumption society is really a kind of "quasi-consumption" by which fuels are converted into heat and physical residues. Even durable goods, such as cars, television sets, and refrigerators, are not really "consumed." Raw materials are put into a more useful form in which people keep them for a certain period. Eventually even these get discarded to scrap heaps for degradation through rusting or oxidation.

The fact of high quasi-consumption in American society, contrasted with the fiction of high consumption, means that human fuel use is never a self-completing process. It is merely one stage in continuous cycles of material transformation and energy flow. The natural processes of ecological production and consumption interact with human energy-using activities in cycles which link the ecosystem to the economy. Because of this link—and the dependency of man on nature which the link presumes—true costs include all energies which the ecosystem must expend to restore equilibrium following the venting of effluents. As man is so frequently the perturbing element, so can he become the corrective agent—but only if the workings of the economy are calibrated to the cycles in the ecosystems with which the economy interacts.

Fuels and their associated effluents can end up in either of two kinds of consumption, or quasi-consumption: (1) use by humans after the price of extracting and delivering the resource has been paid in a market; (2) degradation and assimilation—i.e., "ecological consumption"—through uptake in natural cycles, for which a price also often must be paid in dissipation of the ecosystem. Raw resources must occur in sufficient concentration to justify their exploitation in the first place. It also goes without saying that a complex economy requires transport of the resource from mine or wellhead to a market where consumers can acquire it. These two features of the energy economy—*concentration*, and transportation or *coupling*—are mirrored in the ecosystem.

Like exploitable raw resources, the effluents associated with energy extraction and conversion tend to remain concentrated. Land degradation in Appalachia by mine spoil and city air pollution are two examples of localized problems. Such effluents produced during extraction or conversion must be transported from their points of venting if they are to be acquired for ecological consumption by nature. Thus, a heap of gobbed out earth from a coal mine remains an eyesore—and an affront to the local ecosystem. But if the heap were thinned and graded, reclamation by assimilation into the soil could occur. Similarly, a concentrated haze of air pollutants offends all who must breathe city air. But if winds "sweep" the urban skies, contaminants are carried off and diluted below a threshold of harm.

Given adequate coupling of producing to potentially consuming ecosystems by suitable transport mechanisms, wastes can often be introduced to the ecological cycles at places and in amounts which permit their natural uptake. Thus the ecosystem furnishes a basic model for the humanly engineered energy economy. Reciprocally, such economically relevant processes as resource concentration, transportation, and consumption all have counterparts in the ecosystem. *A key to environmental quality lies in the way that the burden of performing these processes is divided between man and nature, between the artificial economy and the ecosystem.*

Keeping the environmental burden of energy-associated externalities at an acceptable level requires that wastes which are discharged across the economy-ecosystem interface do not unduly disrupt the natural cycles. Nature is under a persistent burden to complete the process of quasi-consumption by assimilating such discharged residues. What man does not consume, nature eventually will. As Athelstan Spilhaus, a former president of the American Association for the Advancement of Science, put the point:

> Industry so far is doing only half its job. It performs magnificent feats . . . to take things from the land, refine them, and mass-manufacture, mass-market and mass-distribute them to the so-called consumer; then the same mass of material is left, after use, to the so-called public sector, to be

"disposed of." By and large, in our society, the private sector makes the things before *use* and the public sector disposes of them *after* use.

Pollution occurs because the tolerance of our "public sinks" is increasingly exceeded.

It need not be thus. If the natural assimilative capacities of the receiving ecosystem are adequate to the load discharged to it, then residues, effluents, and wastes will be degraded or diluted to harmless levels. The ecosystem will maintain a self-cleaning steady-state. If not, ecological coupling through either natural or man-made transport media can often pass on any overload to linked ecosystems which will assimilate excess residues. What matters are the *rates* of discharge, and the *distribution* of residues, relative to the environment's capacity to "consume" them. (A formal discussion of the quasi-consumption and pollutive build-up concepts appears in the Appendix.)

To say that the man-made energy economy functionally parallels the ecosystem is to say that the two perform roughly substitutable tasks. Thus the physical processes involved in fuel combustion for heat duplicates (in controlled, speeded-up form) those metabolic processes used by nature to "consume" vented waste fuel through oxidation. The burning of fuel and the assimilation of fuel residues are alike degradative activities. It is possible to think of carrying a human process of energy use right to the point where the remaining consumptive effort can be quickly and safely carried out by the environment—that is, burning enough of the fuel in a controlled manner such that wastes could readily be absorbed after venting. All such points taken together trace out the optimum ecosystem-economy interface, in the sense that a least-cost balance would be achieved between reliance on man's "artificial" and on the ecosystem's "natural" mechanisms of environmental discipline.

Seral Disturbance and Pollution

Any balance between the artificial and the natural other than at the optimum is either unnecessarily costly in pecuniary terms, or else burdensome to the ecosystem. If the artificial is emphasized, elaborate control mechanims may be put into use—pipes, cleaning machines, smoke suppressors, and so forth to prevent venting of wastes—to manage effluents that nature would, by hypothesis, be able to assimilate without damage to the ecosystem.

On the other hand, waste discharges across the ecosystem-economy interface may occur too quickly. Or nature's assimilative capacity at the point of venting may be insufficient, or the couplings between ecosystems needed to disperse the load in poor repair. Then the ecosystem—or rather, a whole series of linked ecosystems—can be dissipated. In consuming the waste, the environment then consumes itself by aging prematurely in a labored attempt at self-cleansing or restoration. Ecosystem aging is a phenomenon not accurately priced in the economic market but one central to ecological dynamics.

A typical ecosystem moves through a succession of states, technically called a "sere." Young systems like new lakes are shown in the lower lefthand corner of an ecological production-consumption diagram (see Fig. 4), since they neither produce nor consume much energetically charged matter in the course of a year. But with time, a lake undergoes "eutrophication," which literally means "good feeding." The ecosystem produces more plankton, which can feed more fish. There are more birds and animals too, to eat the fish. The aquatic system grows in chronological and ecological age, in complexity, and in the amount of matter which must be consumed in order to preserve an ecological balance.

The term "eutrophication" has gained currency because waste discharges to flowing waters has become a widespread practice. We have seen how the drainage of manures and fertilizers into the rivers of Kansas has caused statewide seral disturbance. The impending "death of Lake Erie"—a water body being killed by overfeeding with wastes from cities and industries—has become a baleful prophesy of the environmentally aroused. A degree of natural aging that would have taken some 15 thousand years has occurred, by some estimates, in a few decades of excessive energy input to this shallowest Great Lake. Man failed to control the input, so nature has had to consume it.

Like an aging lake, a growing fuel economy cycles more and

more energy through its heat machines—and also, more residues through its surrounding environmental sinks. Paralleling the ecological dynamics of a natural sere, such a fuel economy must find ways to insure the assimilation of increasing quantities of vented residues. The environment must develop a mature ecological community's high rate of respiration in order to metabolize the wastes, since only a more mature ecosystem has the assimilative capacity needed to degrade high waste levels. Ecosystem aging must accelerate by means of an alteration in the natural rate of ecological succession. Such alteration is termed "seral disturbance," a phenomenon which adds to depletive waste as a non-pecuniary cost of undisciplined energy use. Some seral disturbance, at least locally, seems as much a cost of energy as is the market price of fuel, even though the two costs cannot be compared on a common dimension.

If, even as the receiving ecosystem ages to increase the environment's ability to consume residues, the discharge continues to exceed nature's assimilative capacity, excess effluents can build to the toxic level—killing life forms and setting back an ecological sere. This occurs, for instance, when a severe oil spill chokes an aquatic ecosystem to death. The resulting build-up of wastes in excess of the environment's ability either to absorb them (through increased respiration) or to disperse them (through naturally diluting transport mechanisms) is properly termed "pollution."

Summary: An Ecologically Meaningful Cost Account

Chapter 1 discussed the reasons for looking beyond the market and its central mechanism, the pecuniary price system, for a sound appraisal of energy costs. Chapters 2 and 3 have presented some basic ecological principles which suggest three cost categories to supplement pecuniary price:

Depletive Waste. The exhaustion of the resource base by irrevocable, inefficient use of nature's energetic investment.

Seral Disturbance. The adverse impact of fuel extraction and conversion on ecosystem aging.

Pollutive Build-up. The accumulation of effluents in a given locale above harmful levels because they overtax the environment's assimilative capacities.

These categories presume an ecological framework in which materials and energy are seen to flow from ecosystem to economy, and vice versa. The causes of seral disturbance and pollution alike lie in poorly attended or poorly regulated flows, in excessive discharges of wastes from the economy to the ecosystem, as in the run-off from feedlots and grainlands to the open waters of Kansas. By the same sign, the corrective to environmental despoliation lies in intelligent management of flows across the ecosystem-economy interface.

REFERENCES

The chapter epigraph comes from p. 6 of the Carson book (1962), as does, indeed, much of the sympathy for an "ecological perspective" expressed in this chapter. Also used were Edward Kormondy, *Concepts of Ecology* (1969), esp. Ch. 2 and 5; National Academy of Science-National Research Council Report 1400, *Waste Management and Control* (1966); and Lamont Cole, "The Ecosphere," April 1958 *Scientific American.* The related "quasi-consumption" concept is based on a seminal paper by Robert Ayres and Allen Kneese in the July 1969 *American Economic Review.*

Statistics used in the agricultural pollution example on p. 65 come from Richard Wagner, *Environment and Man* (1971), pp. 114–15 and Barry Commoner, *The Closing Circle* (1971), pp. 149–150.

The Spilhaus quote on p. 70 comes from the March 1970 *Science*, p. 1673.

No reference section on systematic ecology is complete without an avowal of intellectual debt to the Odums, Eugene and Howard. As indicated at p. 64, the basic "energy budget" and "energy balance" approach traces to work by Eugene P. Odum. See especially his *Ecology* (1966) and Howard T. Odum's *Environment, Power and Society* (1971). An energy balance computation relevant to the theme of this chapter appears in the Odums' "Natural Areas as Necessary Components of Man's Total Environment," in 1972 *Transactions of the North America Wildlife Conference*, furnished in pre-publication draft by the authors.

Supplementing the Odum framework and illustrating energy flow concepts for other types of ecosystems are Clifford Geertz, "Two Types of Ecosystems," Dwain Parrack, "The Bioenergetics of Rural West Bengal," and Richard Lee, "Kung Bushmen Subsistence: An Input-Output Analysis," all in A. P. Vayda, ed., *Environmental and Cultural Behavior* (1969).

Reclamation by Nature of Strip Mined Land. Ridges of "orphan spoil" trace corduroy patterns throughout Appalachia. In time, scrub forests begin to take root and the ecosystem reclaims such land, but unless aided by human restoration efforts, full reclamation takes decades or even generations. (U.S. Department of Agriculture, Gordon S. Smith, and Bureau of Mines.)

. . . for a hundred and thirty years [Appalachia] has exported its resources, all of which—timber, coal, and even crops—have had to be wrested violently from the earth. The nation has siphoned off hundreds of millions of dollars' worth of its resources while returning little of lasting value. For all practical purposes the [Cumberland] plateau has long constituted a colonial appendage of the industrial East and Middle West . . .

Harry Caudill,
Night Comes to the Cumberlands

4

Appalachian Reckoning: The Environmental Costs of Coal

With the arousal in the 1960's and 1970's of widespread ecological concern, belief in the thoroughgoing "connectedness" of things has become commonplace. The assumption of universal connectedness often leads to a vague notion of one big nationwide (or even global) ecosystem in which "everything affects everything else." This grand system is then described as polluted if any localized waste build-ups occur.

Rather than viewing the environment in such undiscriminat-

ing terms, it is preferable to think of a network of small linked
or coupled ecosystems. As discussed in Chapter 3, these ecosystems have different characteristics and capacities (e.g., "productive" versus "assimilative," or young versus mature systems). Environmental problems depend not only on the amount of waste
injected to a receiving ecosystem but also on the adequacy of
that ecosystem's coupling to other systems, or in some cases on
the completeness of its decoupling from the rest of the environment. Adequate coupling may offer an environmental safety
valve. Excess effluents can then be passed on to a nearby ecosystem. On the other hand, the ability to decouple one system
from another may save neighboring areas from unmanageable
loads—keeping most of a region pristine, albeit sometimes at
the cost of severe degradation to the locale which decoupling
isolates.

Because adequate coupling often can disperse polluting effluents to less burdened ecosystems, *the environmental quality
problem lies as much in maldistribution as in overproduction of
wastes*. This generalization is well illustrated by the localized
externalities encountered in the extraction of coal. The Appalachian case (including parts of Pennsylvania), covering about
70% of the nation's coal output, is especially well publicized
and pertinent.

Subsidence and Acid Drainage

Underground coal mining accounts for 60% of recovered bituminous fuel. Such "deep mining" has caused 77% of the nation's more than 8 million undermined acres, equal to the combined sizes of Maryland and Delaware. An article in the *New
York Times* described the resulting problem in one Appalachian
locale:

> From Forest City [Pennsylvania] south almost to Harris-
> burg, the mined out, densely populated land is falling into
> a maze of abandoned tunnels, some of them 150 years old,
> that underlie 10 counties and 484 square miles in as many
> as 12 separate layers.

The collapsed home in Fig. 7 illustrates a principal—but by no means the only—tangible cost of subsidence.

Subsidence is, in a sense, itself a process of ecological restoration, with the earth shifting to a new equilibrium following disturbance of the natural order by deep mining. Because of the ecosystem's tendency to seek equilibrium, all underground mining is liable to cause eventual settling unless worked-out shafts are filled with material of supporting properties equivalent to those of the gobbed out earth. Such backfilling is expensive and

FIGURE 7

Effects of Mine Subsidence

A home in Appalachia collapses as the overburden on which it stands subsides into an abandoned, unsupported deep mine shaft. (Bureau of Mines, Department of Interior.)

time-consuming. But neglect is even costlier. Every dollar spent in one subsidence control project at Wilkes-Barre, Pennsylvania, saved $8 in damage and post-subsidence repair.

The cumulative—and seemingly inevitable—nature of subsidence damage has drawn increased attention to this external cost of deep coal mining. One study, by the TRW Systems Group, reported that 158 thousand acres of urban land had undergone noticeable subsidence by mid-1970, and projected that an additional 3 to 5 million acres across the nation will become exposed to possible subsidence by the year 2000. Against this threat, anti-subsidence insurance—selling a householder half the coal under his property at about 36 ¢ per ton, so it will be left in place to support the overburden—would carry a $630 million premium cost. This figure covers only populated areas. It ignores harm to underground hydraulic systems or to soil stability. Another calculation set $395 million as the cost of foundation-strengthening for buildings on urban land already affected by undermining. Thus a $1 billion estimate—some $400 million for foundation-shoring, the remainder for insurance premiums—seems a low figure for the pecuniary losses to subsidence-associated surface effects.

Disorganization of rock strata during deep mining also upsets the region's water table. Water flowing through underground fractures picks up toxic substances, eventually discharging them to the open ecosystem. Such discharges cause coal mining's second major external cost—acid drainage. According to TRW, some 11 thousand stream miles and 15 thousand acres of impounded water each year absorb more than 4 million tons of equivalent sulfuric acids in 500 billion gallons of mine drainage. An Interior Department Working Committee allocated 75% of such acid drainage in the mid-1960's to deep mining, with strip mining accounting for the remainder. When acidic and alkaline substances are in exact balance, an index known as the "pH measure" will be at 7. The Working Committee found that discharges in intensively worked areas reduce the acidity-basicity of Appalachian streams from a natural 6 or 7 pH to a pH of 5—at which game fish start to die—and down as low as pH counts near 2. Almost 80% of strip mine spoil banks registered pH 3 to 5, with pH 4 lethal to most plants.

The local ecosystem could readily assimilate moderate acid drainage through dilution or neutralization. Fairly high concentrations of bicarbonate—a natural neutralizer for acid pollution —characterize streams through a belt from Ohio to Western Virginia. Other Appalachian streams have low alkalinity, but still enough to "consume" acid in weaker concentrations. Yet the Interior Department committee estimated that 10% of the acid drainage injected into upstream tributaries remains unneutralized by the time that these smaller streams join the larger Appalachian rivers. Assuming that such small streams are virtually "written off" as sinks for mine drainage, this percentage suggests the rate by which untreated coal-associated acid wastes exceed Appalachia's natural assimilative capacity.

The same figure suggests that it is not necessary artificially to restore all mine flowage to perfect neutralization, especially where the stream system couples a mine to major waterways capable of rapidly diluting the effluent to a nontoxic level.

In a mix of techniques lies the pattern suggested as most frequently desirable from an ecological perspective—*use of the environment's capacities to consume wastes up to the limits of the ecosystem's cycles, perhaps permitting some additional localized waste buildups* (as in the upper streams which receive the primary acid drainage load) *so long as such accelerated degradation can be isolated from neighboring ecosystems.* Artificial control measures, ultimately reflected in increased pecuniary prices, thus become factors only *after* the environment's natural sink capacity is used up.

Acid drainage can be handled by: (1) decoupling offending mines from their surroundings, thus segregating the effluent; (2) increasing the assimilation of the effluent by supplementing natural uptake with man-made acid-neutralizing devices; (3) improving the coupling of mine areas to the neighboring ecosystem, thus decreasing the effluent's localization by increasing its dilution; or (4) a mixture of coupling and decoupling, of localization and dilution, of natural consumption and human control. Fig. 8 illustrates the first three techniques.

Decoupling could take the form of water-flow diversion or mine sealing at almost 60 thousand abandoned coal mines. (See Table 3.) According to Federal Water Pollution Control Author-

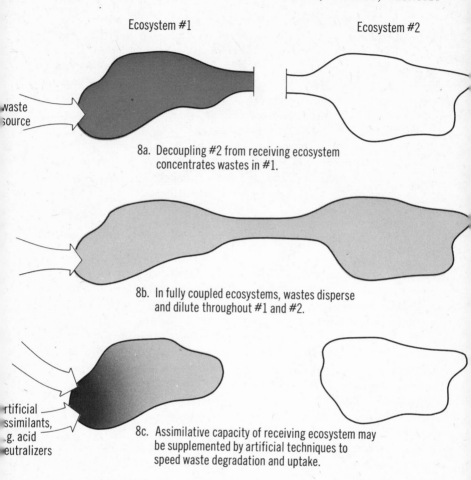

Ecosystem #1   Ecosystem #2

waste
source

8a. Decoupling #2 from receiving ecosystem
    concentrates wastes in #1.

8b. In fully coupled ecosystems, wastes disperse
    and dilute throughout #1 and #2.

artificial
assimilants,
e.g. acid
neutralizers

8c. Assimilative capacity of receiving ecosystem may
    be supplemented by artificial techniques to
    speed waste degradation and uptake.

FIGURE 8

Three Techniques of Waste Control in Coupled Ecosystems

ity analyses, surface diversion (varying from $300 to $3 thousand per acre treated) could reduce mine run-off by as much as
75% —or by as little as 25%. Mine sealing to prevent acid flows
has an even larger variance: from 10% to 80% expected success,
at $1 to $20 thousand per seal.

TABLE 3

Coal Mine Abandonments and Fires, 1969 [a]

	Underground Mines, Abandon or Inactive	Underground and Virgin Bed Fires	Burning Coal Refuse Banks
West Virginia	20,616	16	213
Pennsylvania	7,824	82	142
Virginia	14,397	2	27
Kentucky	12,045	4	49
Illinois	1,605	—	14
Ohio	2,187	6	13
Indiana	960	—	2
	59,634	110	460

[a] *Source:* Bureau of Mines, "Environmental Effects of Underground Mining and Mineral Processing" (1969).

Where decoupling is uneconomical or ineffective, the ecosystem's natural consumptive capacity may be artificially supplemented. Assuming that land is available for sludge disposal, the cost of treating excess Appalachian acid drainage (at 1 ton sulfuric acid for 10 tons of coal), using limestone neutralization with catalytic oxidation, has been estimated at $40 million annually. A Pennsylvania-sponsored test project in 1965 found that lime neutralization and oxygen aeration upgraded water at a 5 thousand ton per day deep mine from pH 2.6 to 7.6. These gains cost $1.09 per thousand gallons of water processed, slightly more than 5¢ per ton of clean coal.

However, more recent reports suggest that this estimate benefited from local peculiarities in the mine used for the experiment. These reports find 2 thousand gallons of acid water produced for every ton of coal mined in typical Appalachian mines, leading to a much higher total cost of complete treatment—in the neighborhood of $2 per ton or $1.1 billion annually. The TRW estimate, if spread over 560 million tons mined by all means in 1969, would add about 7¢ or 1–2 percent of the minehead price at late 1960's levels. The higher estimate would boost coal prices by 20%. Thus a midway figure of $500 million per year in the early 1970's seems a reasonable first approximation of charges to coal for acid drainage.

Coal Mining and Land Degradation

Coal mines also produce solid waste—adding to some 18.5 billion tons of refuse from all sources in 2 thousand waste piles covering 1.8 million acres throughout the nation.

As indicated in Table 3, in 1969 at least 110 fires were burning out of control in abandoned mines or virgin coal beds, plus four times this number in refuse banks. Some 2.3 million persons, 80% of them in Pennsylvania, suffer continuous damage to health, property, and environment from these mine-waste fires.

Again, cost estimation is difficult. A 1967 Interior Department publication, "Mine Fires," reports that it cost $443 thousand to bring one 23-acre underground fire near North Scranton, Pennsylvania, under control. Applying the same figure to one hundred mine fires, and only one-fourth of this per-job cost to four hundred smoldering refuse banks, gives almost $90 million as an estimate for needed repair costs. This pecuniary figure probably covers only a small fraction of the yearly damage costs of uncontrolled burning throughout Appalachia. In 1969, Pennsylvania alone committed $70 million in conjunction with the Bureau of Mines just to control fires from mines for which clear corporate liability had lapsed. Thus a $150 million mine-fire cost seems an understated figure.

More serious than mine fires are the two other main externalities associated with land disturbance—unsightly, largely unusable mounds of waste earth, often rimming strip mine pits; and soil erosion, which combines with acid flows to compound a growing water pollution problem in coal country.

The most pervasive evidence of environmental degradation is not the much publicized surface mine. Strip mines cover less than 1% of Appalachia's 117 million acres. They also tend to be worked out of direct sight from the main travel arteries. The most visible effects of unreclaimed land are the region's fouled, turbid waterways. These linked problems—waste earth, with worsening water pollution from erosion off the same mounds—illustrate a prime irony in the relationship between coal extraction and the ecosystem. Earth wastes themselves are highly localized, almost immobile. This immobility inhibits reclamation, since "natural assimilation" of dirt piles requires movement—thinning and grading to restore the land's natural contour. On the other hand, water as an instrument of erosion can prove *too* effective a transport medium, carrying dirt off to foul an entire series of linked waterways.

The need, then, is to decouple erosion-prone earth waste mounds from more distant river-linked ecosystems through grading and planting. The same practices hold the answer to reclamation of earth waste near the mine.

The earth waste problem will get worse unless minehead discipline makes it better. The Bureau of Mines reported that 435 million tons were mechanically cleaned at mines in 1969. More than 100 million tons, 23%, were discharged as refuse—adding to the load of earth waste and mine spoil. Pressures for clean air will prompt cleaning of ever higher percentages of raw coal, including lower grades which yield more refuse. Furthermore, TRW reported:

> In Pennsylvania, the Pittsburgh bed has been depleted from an original deposit of 14 billion tons to less than 4 billion tons which is considered ultimately recoverable. These reserves are presently being depleted at the rate of 30 million tons annually under greater cover (1500 feet maximum) with extremely gaseous conditions, high in sulfur content and lower in quality than that part of the bed already depleted. The same generally applies to the majority of our reserves.

Thus all trends suggest that the typical load of coal brought to market will yield ever higher tonnages of waste, some to erode off into area waterways, and much of the rest to stay as unsightly heaps.

Waste which is not eroded into streams must in time be reabsorbed into the lithosphere or covered over by the biosphere through revegetation. Natural assimilation back into the ecosystem must occur within a few miles (or even feet) of the mine. But the immediate ecosystem must also support the mine itself, which—as indicated in Chapter 3—cannot absorb wastes so long as it is being worked. And the locale must support the workers, with their families and their servicing economy. Thus *earth waste near intensive coal production sites models the situation to be expected more generally in a crowded future where environmental productive and assimilative capacities are both overtaxed and in direct competition with each other.* In Appalachia, this competition is a matter of history rather than of conjecture. And the ecosystem's assimilative capacities seem to be losing.

The loamy character of two-thirds of Appalachian soil is congenial to quick plant coverage, always assuming a non-lethal acidity level. Ideally, a spoil bank will be leached of acid, neutralizing the top-soil for revegetation, in 3 to 5 years. But during those years, increased erosion is likely to carry off the surface soil as quickly as percolative leaching reduces acidity. Thus the bank continuously presents a new surface, invariantly acidic and resistant to cultivation. As a result, the Working Committee found that only about 60% of stripped sites regained some natural vegetation, suggesting that the typical Appalachian ecosystem's natural assimilative capacities are *exceeded* by about two-thirds.

Even where assimilation seems to succeed, "natural" reclamation of mine spoil cannot guarantee restoration of scenic qualities, repair of water table disruptions, or prevention of long-term erosion. The contribution of coal mining erosion to water pollution is not precisely calculable, but it is known to be considerable, both in absolute tonnage and relative to the ecosystem's assimilative capacities. Thus the locale loses in two ways—through the loss of potentially useful land, and through pollution of waters. Moreover, Appalachia's regional waterways are already laboring under a heavy load of sediment from other sources, such as an active road-building program.

The Working Committee estimated some 18 thousand miles of strip mine contours in Appalachia, affecting about 30 acres per mile. Along 5 thousand miles, spoil had merely been pushed off the minebench to cascade downslope, eventually into Appalachian streams. These waterways then become the coupling agents whereby an initially localized problem—earth waste—spreads to other ecosystems such that, overall, the Working Committee estimated at least 1 additional acre adversely affected for every acre actually stripped. Based on U.S. Forest Service studies, the Committee estimated 640 tons of soil per square mile as typical annual erosion in undisturbed forested areas of Kentucky's coal belts. U.S. Geological Survey and Commonwealth of Kentucky measurements indicate ten times this erosion from stripped sections.

As eroded sediments eventually come out of suspension, they get reassimilated by the lithosphere, often clogging the stream channel. The Working Committee reported that 60% of headwater streams showed reduced flow capacities (thus reducing the water volume available to dilute acid drainage in the bargain). As a result, the silt load passed on to larger rivers is about 25% of the original eroded tonnage—another measure of the environmental overload in Appalachia due to coal mining.

Pursuing the research of the working Committee, Interior Department analysts in 1967 estimated that more than 1 million acres urgently need "Limited Basic Reclamation" at $304 million. Another 2 million acres should have additional planting and grading, for an estimated cumulative cost of $757 million. Against these requirements, actual industry investment in reclamation during the mid-1960's approached $6.5 million per year. Averaged over the 123 million ton output by surface mining in 1964, this outlay added about 5.5¢ to a ton of coal.

As surface mining's environmental effects are for the most part localized, so do the difficulties of reclamation vary from locale to locale. In 1971, well after public attention had been focused on the environmental damage of strip mining, the nation's largest coal user, Tennessee Valley Authority, estimated a more than threefold variation in reclamation costs—from $150 to $500 per acre. Such estimates are keyed to local statutory requirements, and do not necessarily imply restoration of ecological conditions before disturbance. European experience suggests closer to a $1 per ton extra cost if full environmental restoration is to be achieved. Such an "environmental quality surcharge" would, in fact, bring the $4 per ton mine-head price of surface-mined coal in 1970 just about exactly into line with the $5 per ton industry average for all coal. By rough TVA calculations, a $1 per ton surcharge for surface-mined coal would add 5% to the price of electricity marketed by that corporation, or some

$30 million annually to coal costs computed without regard to environmental quality.

Taking a more conservative figure of 75¢ per ton, at an annual surface mining production of about 200 million tons, gives a $150 million estimate of needed reclamation costs over and above the almost $1 billion dollar bill (adjusting for higher 1970's prices) due for accumulated back damage.

Summary: Coal's Environmental Debt

Subsidence, acid drainage, earth waste and erosion, and scenic degradation reveal Appalachia's intensive development as the nation's main coal area. Not all of these environmental costs are externalized. Nor are all of their effects free of attempts at reclamation. Yet cumulatively, they have built to a substantial ecological debt. A reckoning, not to say full repayment, is long overdue.

The total figure doubtless exceeds $2.8 billion in Appalachia alone, most of it in cumulative damages—more than one-third of it from subsidence, at least $500 million from acid drainage, $150 million in mine fire control, and a bare minimum of $1.15 billion for earth waste reclamation and soil conservation. Adjusting for the 30% of bituminous and lignite mined outside of Appalachia each year, and assuming that damage histories in these other areas are roughly proportionate, gives a $4 billion total.

This charge is an insurance-plus-repair bill for both projected and cumulative damage. Still, it is likely an understated figure. If spread over 1 trillion therms of coal consumption—the 1969 *Minerals Yearbook* latest one-year estimate multiplied by 5—in order to give a half decade to amortize the costs of back damage repair, pecuniarily measurable externalities through the mid-1970's would add about 4 mills to the cost of a therm. A therm equals 100 thousand Btu's.

Assuming a 4.1¢ per therm market price of coal (including transportation) over the period of amortization, this add-on would represent about 10% of the base price. But of course the reckoning cannot end with a purely pecuniary total. For instance, the relatively high subsidence cost—measured in dollar terms—may be deceptive. Subsidence occurs where insurance, real estate, and construction markets actively operate. These factors make pecuniary appraisal easier than with the other coal-associated externalities. Yet in the long run, and in *real* terms, damage to the ecosystem may be more costly.

Thus, mine acid discharges exceed the ecosystem's natural absorptive ability by at least 10%. Spoil banks multiply erosion by a factor of 10, worsening both land degradation and stream siltation. The production of waste mounds requires reduction by about one-third. And even selective reduction of earth waste— concentrating on the most acidic, erosion-prone areas—might not insure the minimum 25% cutback in erosion volumes needed to prevent continued mine-associated sedimentation of Appalachia's major waterways. Difficulties in translating such damage into pecuniary terms helps hide from a market-oriented society coal mining's full range of externalities.

Also helping to hide the true costs of coal mining is the concentration of adverse environmental effects. Coal's costs— whether best appreciated in pecuniary or in ecological terms— share one dominant characteristic: *the main environmental damages are not only externalized but localized in the producing rather than in the consuming ecosystems.* For example, mine spoil affronts the environment at the very source of raw fuel. Hence the costs of earth waste, unless internalized by forcing mine operators to bear full reclamation costs, are not necessarily brought home to a distant purchaser of the fuel whose production occasioned the residues. "Localization of effects" has become a characteristic of polluted or despoiled regions. Thus environmental degradation tends to be discriminatory, unfairly burdening those in the vicinity of the discharge, though they may not be major consumers or even beneficiaries of the resource being exploited—a point which applies most strongly to Appalachia.

The tendency of environmental damage to be localized, in conjunction with the fact that the costs of coal-associated externalities are small relative to overall industry revenues, suggests a need to focus on redistributing these costs rather than merely on reducing their magnitude. The needed redistribution of costs —whether in money or in kind—can be accomplished in two ways: *pecuniarily*, by internalizing the costs of fuel extraction so consumers, rather than persons in the extractive locale, bear the burden; and *ecologically*, by exercising better control over rates of effluent discharges and over the couplings between actually and potentially affected ecosystems, so full benefit can be taken of nature's assimilative capacities.

REFERENCES

The chapter epigraph comes from p. 325 of the cited book (1962), and Caudill's estimate of European coal reclamation costs, used at p. 87, from a communication in the January 28, 1971, *New York Times*.

The quote at p. 78 appeared in the September 20, 1969, *New York Times*. The study by TRW, relied on extensively for subsidence and acid drainage damage estimates, was submitted as Report #13497-6001-RO-00 by the Thompson-Ramo-Woodbridge Systems Group to the Office of Science and Technology, Executive Office of the President, on June 1970, under the title, *Underground Coal Mining in the United States*. The subsidence cost referenced on p. 80 comes from an Interior Department—Commonwealth of Pennsylvania pamphlet called "Operation Backfill" (1964). It is available through the Bureau of Mines, Department of Interior, as are the study of acid drainage by James Boyer of Bituminous Coal Research, Inc. cited on p. 83 and the 1969 study by Bureau staff members entitled "Environmental Effects of Underground Coal mining." The FWPCA estimates at p. 82 are taken from this report.

The Pennsylvania-sponsored acid drainage study was conducted by Dow-Oliver, Inc., and is reported in 10 *American Chemistry Society Reports, Division of Fuel Chemistry*, No. 1.

The Pennsylvania fire control figure was reported in the September 29, 1969 *New York Times*.

On surface mining effects, Appalachian Working Committee Report to the Secretary of Interior (June 30, 1966), "Study of Strip and Surface Mining in Appalachia," as well as the cited 1967 analysis, entitled "Surface Mining and Our Environment," are both available from the Interior Department. The cost estimates for reclamation cited on p. 87 come from pp. 82–83 of the latter publication. The mechanical coal-cleaning statistic and the actual minehead costs of coal were taken from the Bureau of Mines' September 18, 1970 Coal Report. All figures relating to TVA were supplied by Messrs. Aubrey and Evans of that organization, as indicated in the Acknowledgments.

Elements of the Energy Order: Pipelines and Tanker. South American oil moves by pipe to boat for transport to an east coast refinery. Minimizing leaks and spills at each transfer point is necessary for pollution control. Standard Oil Company (New Jersey).

. . . as things stand, the petroleum industry sits on top of the world and likes the *status quo* very much, perhaps a little too much. And yet, it is to be hoped that in its collective wisdom the industry will reach the conclusion that ours is an interdependent world, and that none, not even those at the top, can long gain from policies that fall short of the maximum promotion of the common weal.

Erich Zimmermann,
Conservation in the Production of Petroleum

5

Petroleum Out of Place

~~~~~~~~~~~~~~~~~~~~~~~~~~~~~~~

Some of the most widely publicized pollution episodes occur following extraction, during fuel transportation and processing. A tanker spill or a pipeline break wastes oil to the environment rather than moving it to market for sale. Thus the artificial network for containing petroleum gets coupled to the wrong consuming ecosystem. The spill produces a growing pool of a "resource out of place."

Fig. 9 on the next page illustrates the main categories of breach in the interface that, ideally, separates the artificial control network in the oil economy from the natural ecosystem. Any venting of oil through one of these breaks in the interface—either by accident or purposely, as in disposal of waste oils and sludges—may threaten to pollute the receiving water or air medium. Moreover, an affront to one medium may ultimately degrade the other. Thus evaporation of spilled oil couples the hydrospheric reservoir to the atmosphere. This creates an

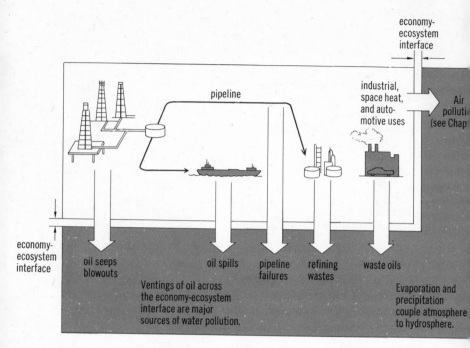

FIGURE 9

Oil Pollution Across the Ecosystem-Economy Interface

ecological link between water and air pollution. Experiments in Alaska's oil-rich Cook Inlet indicate that volatile oil fractions—especially gasolines and kerosenes—evaporate within eight hours. They may thereafter cycle back and forth between atmosphere and hydrosphere, just as noxious gases may ride with the turbulence over a city, never fully diluting.

The Concept of the Energy Order

The concept of pollution as caused by a resource out of place presumes a system where resources, including fuels and their effluents, *do* belong at each phase in their exploitation. Thus, the idea of disorder assumes some notion of order—of a planned, working "energy order." This energy order concept may be developed as a framework for energy-policy analysis while considering the environmental impact of the most mobile—and currently most important—fuel form, petroleum (both oil and gas).

The energy order is the most important physical embodiment of the nation's fuel economy. It is the elaborate network of man-made coupling devices through which fuels—and fuel-associated effluents—move from place to place. The primary function of the energy order is to keep fuel "in place," maximizing its usefulness and minimizing waste or environmental harm. No leaks or interruptions should occur, since it is the integrity of this physical shell which produces the "order."

Ideally, all energy movements would occur within the shell— mine timbers and rail cars to keep or get coal where it is wanted; pipelines to move petroleum; shielding devices to segregate radioactivity from the environment; the nation's electric grid, from high voltage wires to local distribution conduits. Pollution can result from a failure in the physical integrity of the energy order—sometimes by the rupture of a physical casing, as in well blowouts or pipeline failures; sometimes with uncontrolled venting of a noxious effluent following combustion (e.g., air pollution). Such a failure in the energy order *diffuses* a resource or waste to the environment.

Obversely, the energy order is *concentrative*. Resources must be moved to market in sufficient concentrations to justify their exploitation. Just as nature's deposition of a raw resource in concentrated pools facilitates its discovery and extraction, concentration by artificial means—by the energy order—facilitates control of the fuel after extraction. Transportation of a resource from a coal seam or wellhead to market is itself a process of dynamic control—insuring that the fuel will change location according to a spatial plan (the route of the mine shaft, pipeline, or tanker) and schedule (the fuel's required rate of flow to meet demand).

If an effluent can be concentrated, as by maintenance of integrity in the energy order, it can often be made harmless through human control. The more concentrated a substance, the easier it normally is to "get a grip" on it for handling. Thus, an ability to transport potentially damaging substances is necessary to segregate them from areas where they will do harm. But an ability to segregate resources both in space and in time—that is, to concentrate them—is also necessary in order to transport them.

These principles are well illustrated by following oil from its extraction through the tanker-pipeline networks which carry it for processing and ultimate marketing.

The Extractive Phase: Oil Blowouts and Seeps

A 1968 study sponsored by the American Petroleum Institute (but conducted by an independent research firm) indicated a 22% industry-wide increase in capital investment for water conservation between 1966 and 1967—up to $54 million—and a 19% increase for improved operations and maintenance in crude oil production. The National Petroleum Council's June 1971 "Environmental Conservation" report estimates industry expenditures on water quality control at more than $1 billion in the period 1966 through 1970. This investment figure exceeds that spent on the more salient air pollution problem.

While such steps move toward internalizing pollution abatement costs, it is impossible to develop a perfect hedge against environmental despoliation.

Oil commonly is brought to the surface mixed with briny water. This brine, often in volumes exceeding that of the oil by a factor of 3, may be pumped back underground—the disposition of 72% of oil-associated waters. Alternatively, the brine may be evaporated from lined pits or piped to nonpotable water bodies, techniques which together account for another 24%. Some coastal pollution doubtless occurs with oceanic disposal, since it is impossible to strip all oil from waste water before venting. Additionally, dissolved oils in discarded drilling muds may eventually seep through to local ground-water systems, thence to be carried away from the oil field.

But in the main, oil pollution is not a serious externality in on-shore drilling. The costs of interference with the local ecosystem may be internalized, since in principle such damages are reflected in the lease price of the land being drilled, and are thus passed on to customers.

But growing energy demand, in conjunction with restrictions on imports of foreign crude, has pushed oil exploration off-shore. Potential ecological as well as pecuniary costs increase with off-shore drilling.

In twenty-five years, some 10.4 thousand oil and gas wells have been drilled off United States shores, mostly in the Gulf of Mexico and off Southern California. Blowouts or seeps from such rigs can foul marine surroundings for miles, and perhaps for years. Yet even with the most serious incidents, harm mainly befalls the relatively few who happen to live in or do business in the area where a blowout chances to occur. Thus, as with the coal-associated effects covered in Chapter 4, *the overriding environmental feature of oil well disasters is a relative localization of effects.*

Unlike acid drainage or erosion from earth waste, blowouts are not continuous "side effects" of oil extraction. The most serious cases occur episodically, with dramatic infrequency and unpredictable consequences. U.S. Geological Survey records show 22 blowouts for the more than 9 thousand off-shore wells on which histories are available. Fewer than 50% of these are charged with having caused pollution, property damage, or personal injury. Moreover, advances in the off-shore drilling arts are thought to reduce hazards for the future. Nevertheless, the 2.5 per thousand well blowout figure suggests a possible incident each year.

In January 1969, a well owned by Union Oil in the channel between Santa Barbara, California and Catalina Island began to leak. Reservoir pressures tend to be high in the rich Santa Barbara off-shore oil field, and the sinking of the well destabilized the channel bottom sufficiently for the pressures to force uncontrolled crude oil to escape. This blowout brought the off-shore danger to public view, suggesting both the dimension of the problem and the incompleteness of control and cost-evaluation techniques. At least 78 thousand barrels leaked to the environment in the spill's first one hundred days—and possibly the true magnitude was ten times that level. (See Fig. 10.) Economists Walter Mead of the University of California at Santa Barbara and Phillip Sorensen of Florida State University calculated the cost to society of the Santa Barbara oil spill at $16.4 million. This included $10.5 million spent by oil companies to control

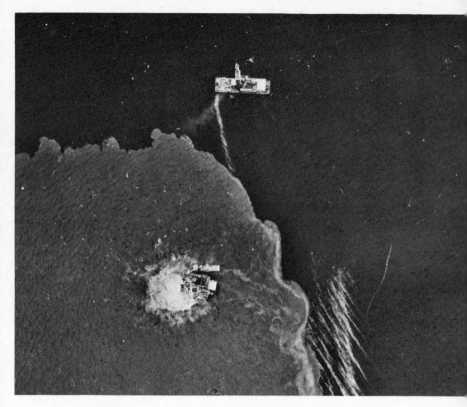

FIGURE 10

The Santa Barbara Oil Blowout

The light-gray area is seeping oil in the Santa Barbara channel surrounding
the well in the center of the photo. (Courtesy of the Environmental Protection
Agency.)

leaking crude and to clean up beaches. Externalized damages to
private property, the fishing industry, marine life, and recreation, plus the value of lost oil, totaled $5.4 million according to
Mead and Sorensen.

But much information was unavailable to Mead and Sorensen,
pending outcome of lawsuits for over $1 billion filed against the
Federal government and the oil companies. Also, the beach
cleaning costs calculated by Mead and Sorensen excluded significant donations of labor and expense by volunteers. The
Mead-Sorensen evaluation of almost 4 thousand birds lost at

$7.4 thousand contrasts with the January 19, 1971 San Francisco Harbor tanker collision record. Following a spill there of up to 1 million gallons, Standard Oil gave $150 thousand to volunteer groups working to save five hundred birds. This suggests a "per bird" value fifty times the Mead-Sorensen estimate, *even if two-thirds of Standard's San Francisco expense is attributed only to public relations*, rather than primarily to the ecological objective of restoring the local biome. Still in all, if the Mead-Sorensen figures are multiplied several times over, they would represent an exceedingly small per barrel increment to oil costs in this multi-billion-dollar industry.

A year after Santa Barbara, in February and March 1970, two more costly blowouts—one with an off-shore fire—imperiled shrimp and oyster beds off Louisiana valued at $100 million. Shell Oil contained the blaze at an estimated cost exceeding $43 million before known damage to the off-shore ecosystem occurred. But as with the Santa Barbara case, where up to 90% mortality hit animals and plants in the worst-affected area, the extent of long term seral disturbance may take years to appraise. If the same (probably understated) ratio of external to internalized dollar costs resulted off Louisiana as Mead and Sorensen estimated for Santa Barbara, a $15 million or so figure would result.

Since off-shore hazards seem an inescapable concomitant of the increasingly extensive exploratory process on which an oil-based economy depends, prevention or clean-up costs should be assigned to the oil-consuming sector as a whole. A per barrel environmental quality surcharge might be added to all oil, whether recovered on-shore, off-shore, or abroad. Charging an "insurance premium" of 5 mills per barrel at an early 1970's yearly United States demand of 5.5 billion barrels, would give almost $28 million annually to deal with major oil blowouts. At 63 therms to the barrel, such a surcharge would add about one-tenth mill to the per therm price of oil.

Oil Spills: A Case Study in Ecological Consumption

If the relative insignificance of the blowout-associated pecuniary add-on is surprising, it is even more surprising that the indicated environmental surcharge remains small for the substantially larger externality category of oil spills from sea-going vessels. Again, contrasts with coal are instructive—in regard both to industry size and to the characteristics of their products.

Accidental discharges of coal to the environment (such as spillage en route from mine to market) do minimum harm, owing to coal's relative immobility and its slow oxidation rate at normal temperatures. But oil is eminently "consumable." When oil is the resource out of place, it will rarely just lie there. It will impose a demand on the affronted ecosystem to assimilate it by absorption in life forms and through dilution over a whole network of coupled ecosystems.

Water pollution by spilled oil divides into three external cost categories: (1) ocean-going discharges which befoul the environment, can accelerate ecological aging, and sometimes lead to persistent pollutive build-ups—but which are difficult to appraise in dollar terms; (2) major coastal spills, mostly from large tankers; and (3) smaller pollutive episodes with nuisance value and possible localized water quality degradation.

Ocean-going Oil Discharges. Some 48 thousand ships of more than 100 gross tons steam the world's seas. About 8% of these —the 4 thousand tanker-class vessels—are thought to cause 50% of water pollution from vented oil, both from spills and from intentional venting in unloading or deballasting. Projections are for more deep-draft tankers to connect overseas petroleum supplies with growing domestic demand—another instance of the energy order, in the form of ships and pipelines, serving to couple producing with consuming ecosystems. With perhaps 60% of annual world oil production moving over water sometime before conversion, a yearly 1 million ton deep-water hydrocarbon discharge through deballasting of oil tankers poses a real threat to the ocean's assimilative capacity, and hence to sea life itself—including the seaborne plankton which recycles carbon dioxide and furnishes four-fifths of the world's oxygen.

In 1962 Shell Oil introduced "load-on-top" deballasting, since adopted by 80% of the world's tankers. Unloaded oil tankers carry water as a ballast. Some oil from prior loads invariably remains, floats to the top of the ballast water, and is skimmed off.

This skimmed oil is kept separate, to be flushed into special sinks after the tanker docks. Thus after skimming, the tanker can deballast at sea by pumping relatively clean water from its tanks and be ready for immediate reloading on reaching port. Now, a 40 thousand ton tanker will discharge 3 tons of oil during sea-going deballasting, compared with 83 tons before load-on-top.

Even with load-on-top, deballasting at sea can overtax the degradative capacities of the seaborne microbes which function as nature's scavengers of vented hydrocarbons.

Scores of bacteria, yeasts, and fungi have been found to oxidize some petroleum fractions. Hence, hydrocarbon injections to the aquatic ecosystem in small amounts may be harmless, and can even be beneficial by feeding microbial oxidizers. In the open sea, given a rich enough culture of such feeding agents, about 1 milligram of oil per liter of water can be oxidized in a day at 73° F. Under optimum conditions organisms can convert, on the average, 35% of the carbon in spilled oil into protein-rich new biomass, in turn furnishing food for predators higher in the trophic pyramid. But since no one species feeds on all fractions, biodegradation needs complex, multi-species, mature ecosystems—a pertinent example of the relevance of ecological concepts to energy-associated waste disposal. And in amounts too large for natural uptake, oil inhibits rather than promotes growth.

As with most other forms of energy-associated effluents, *in order to maximize natural uptake of vented oil, some intervening agency between discharge and assimilation—an ecological link or coupling mechanism—must present the potential contaminant to an ecosystem with excess capacity, in a form and at a rate suitable for natural absorption.* In the case of oil-venting at sea, the key lies in gradual release of ballast waters as close to the ship's propellers as possible. The churning wake can then break up the oil into small globules with large surface areas to be attacked by the sea's degradative agents. Thus by disciplined use of an existing element in the energy industry's capital inventory, the tanker's propellers are appropriated to the energy order as a device both to help control a resource out of place and to increase nature's assimilative capacity.

It has been estimated that there are 1 to 2 thousand bacteria per liter in seawater far offshore, about an order of magnitude smaller than near coastal waters. With care, tanker deballasting can leave oil concentrations of 0.1 to 0.2 parts per million (ppm), well below the biodegradative potential of the oceans. But the oceans have no adequate policing to enforce deballasting discipline. Nor does any working market bring home the ecological costs of deep-water pollution. So in the absence of discipline to reverse decades of affront to the sea, long-term harm to the oceans—and hence to all who depend on their increase—may yet present the children of today's polluters with an unavoidable bill.

Coastal Oil Spills. So far as spills closer to shore are concerned, U.S. Coast Guard statistics on spills in violation of law (including non-vessel-associated) jumped from 192 in 1964, to 371 in 1966, to 714 in 1968—more than half of them caused by literal, physical flaws in the energy order.

In 1968, 277 cases involved vessels. Bursts, leaks, or holes in ships caused the discharges in 140 instances. The remaining 50% of the vessel-associated spills stemmed from judgmental failures to control the resource (e.g., overfilling of oil tanks or undisciplined bilge-pumping).

Incidents near land, including venting incidents originating in on-shore facilities such as refinery complexes, varied from 2 to 7.5 thousand per year in 1966 and 1967. Most such spills release fewer than 1 thousand gallons, averaging between 50 and 100. At 75 gallons per minor incident, 5 thousand small spills gives a working figure of 375 thousand gallons annually—about 9 thousand barrels. Coast Guard statistics for 1969, however, suggest that much larger discharges are commonly associated with water-borne transport of fuel. Tankers and barges vented about 350 thousand barrels in 343 separate incidents. The 1970 estimate from the Coast Guard's Environmental Coordination Branch sets venting episodes at the 358.3 thousand barrel level, with some 1.2 thousand incidents associated with ships as against 1.5 thousand from onshore (e.g., refineries) and off-shore (e.g., submarine pipelines) facilities.

More than 83% of the 1970 incidents polluted coastal waters. Another 8% of the episodes recorded in Coast Guard files occurred in rivers and major inland lakes. Thus spills tend to concentrate close to population centers, where they are most likely to interfere with recreation, foul equipment and threaten waterborne life. The bacterial agents which degrade oil are also most common in these waters (as they are, significantly, endemic in oilfields). But a hydrocarbon molecule needs 3 to 4 times its own weight in oxygen for complete biodegradation, plus a rich bacterial culture to furnish agents of combination and catalysis. The dissolved oxygen in more than 22.5 million gallons of seawater is needed to metabolize one 75 gallon oil spill. This ratio of oxygen to oil severely limits a coastal ecosystem's ability to cleanse itself of a large spill—or even of repeated small ones.

In September 1969, a 178 thousand gallon spill of highly toxic home-heating distilled oil, off West Falmouth, Massachusetts, overwhelmed that ecosystem's biodegradative capacity. Woods Hole Oceanographic Institute researchers found that eight months after the spill, the oil had diluted—while remaining toxic to marine life forms—through a water volume as much as 42 feet deep and over 5 thousand acres of water surface, plus another 500 acres of marsh. This gives about 53 billion gallons of polluted water (including the affected marshland), about 300 thousand times the volume of oil originally spilled.

The well-studied West Falmouth spill illustrates the need to redistribute wastes so the ecosystem's own absorptive capacity can be brought into play. The entire polluted water volume does *not* contribute to biodegradation of the contaminating oil. In such ecologically active near-shore waters, about 4 thousand grams of oil per gallon of seawater can be biodegraded per day. So if each cubic foot of polluted water volume contributed equally to ecological cleaning, the 600 million gram West Falmouth spill would have fully yielded to the ecosystem's restorative activity in less than a single day. This estimate is utterly out of line with the Woods Hole finding of continued killing pollution eight months after the venting. Why?

In accord with the analytical framework suggested at the beginning of Chapter 4, the West Falmouth dynamics are best approached by viewing the waters as a series of coupled small aquatic ecosystems. Spilled oil is initially localized in the slick on top of the water. If the slick is not quickly broken down by biodegradation, evaporation, or human intervention, the oil will be dispersed—some by gravitational settling, some by coating moving creatures, some by incorporation in life forms, some through absorption in porous rocks or driftwood. These incorporators locally concentrate oil. Each concentrator represents, in a sense, a little ecosystem "supersaturated" with oil. As biodegradation proceeds in less severely affected regions, oil keeps seeping out from these concentrators to maintain the balance of saturation pressures throughout a much larger polluted volume of water. Killing continues until porous rocks, carcasses, reeds, and muds are depleted of their pollutive store. Thus the entire volume stays polluted because the water itself serves as a transport medium, coupling the concentrators to portions of the network which have lower concentrations.

For natural uptake and degradation to occur, movement of oil under the pressure of differential concentrations in the polluted water volume must put the contaminant in touch with effective biodegraders. Natural assimilation proceeds in a small fraction of the total polluted volume, mostly near the water surface where oil, microbes, and oxygen readily come together. Assuming biodegradation to occur only in the surface liters of water over West Falmouth's polluted area, break-up of all the oil (now in more dilute form, since it is released at a slower rate by the concentrators) should have taken about nine months. This figure is consistent with the Woods Hole findings.

Meanwhile, the ecosystem suffered a severe, if localized, seral disturbance. Living biomass was cut in half. Pollution killed 85% of the area's aquatic herbivores and carnivores, plus maybe 50% of the ecosystem's original flora. Accompanying these effects was a decrease in West Falmouth's species diversity, in the stability of the depleted aquatic ecosystem, and of course in commercial, recreational, and aesthetic values. Overall, damage was worse than at Santa Barbara, which suffered pollution from less toxic crude oil seeping directly from the well.

Pecuniary Cost of Oil Spills. The Northwest Petroleum Company paid $100 thousand to the town of West Falmouth, and twice that to the Commonwealth of Massachusetts, to cover the value of one year's destroyed shellfish crop. Taking $400 thousand as a conservative estimate of West Falmouth damages ultimately convertible to dollar terms gives roughly $100 in costs per barrel spilled. Satisfaction of some damage claims may, as at West Falmouth, internalize a substantial portion of these costs.

Analysis of the more frequent smaller spills, which are easier to cost-out on a per incident basis, suggests a lower average cost of spillage. A typical 500 gallon harbor spill from a U.S. naval vessel will cost from $1 to $2 thousand to clean, exclusive of labor costs. Battelle Institute studies identified two optimal systems for harbor cleanups, one using a strategy of dispersion and the other, of concentration. Quick use of chemical dispersants costs about $1.15 per gallon of spill; and a containment boom to control oil while it is being removed with a suction device, $1.10 to $2.50 per gallon. Naval discipline, seamanship, and public relations demand prompt clean-up. Thus these figures are likely to represent costs of prompt, fairly complete action to control vented oil.

With a 15 million gallon yearly spillage estimate, a $1.25 per gallon damage or clean-up figure translates into an annual $18.75 million bill for oil spills. More than tripling this figure to $60 million to cover pecuniary underestimation of ecological damages—as well as costs of locating spills, transport of cleaning equipment, and so forth—still leaves a moderate aggregate external cost compared with overall industry revenues. Nor is the relative cost increased by more than a few mills per barrel if the estimate is doubled to $120 million annually, which assumes that non-vessel-associated incidents account for half of coastal oil pollution.

Spreading a $120 million annual charge over a 5.5 billion barrel yearly demand gives about 2.2¢ per barrel. With oil going for $3.16 per barrel at the well, according to the Office of Emergency Preparedness (April 1971), plus maybe 50¢ for transportation to a refinery, this adds less than 1% to the before-processing cost of oil.

Of course, *the same factor which seems to minimize the pecuniary significance of this externality—the huge volume of oil demand over which the cost is spread—prevents minimization of the ecological costs.* Indeed, the volume of oil to be recovered and moved in the 1970's makes accidents almost certain. Fractionally small losses to the industry can still inflict major ecological damage if concentrated in a handful of locales. In such off-shore locales, markets are least likely to be helpful in setting an accurate dollar cost on true damage—even if techniques were available to estimate ecological damage over time to affected biomes. Finally, the problem of computing externalities is further complicated by the oil companies' own tendency to internalize extra preventive and clean-up costs. All of which makes the distinction between pecuniary and ecological costs especially pertinent to oil's most visible kind of environmental threat—even as it makes quantitative application of the same distinction doubly difficult.

Petroleum under Pressure: The Pipeline Dilemma

Some 70% of domestic crude oil and 65% of natural gas moves through the nation's 200 thousand miles of pipeline. Pressures often exceed 1 thousand pounds per square inch, implying an explosive as well as a motive force.

Today urbanization, population, growth, and affluence heighten the value of remaining untouched or "wilderness" areas. Planning new pipeline rights of way through such lands represents a potential affront to increasingly scarce nature preserves—an issue heatedly joined in the controversy over a projected Alaskan pipeline. On the other hand, transporting oil or gas through built-up areas increases the exposure of persons and property to harm in case of a failure in the energy order, e.g., a pipe explosion. The resulting dilemma defines the modern problem of petroleum-transportation planning.

The projected Alaskan pipeline will carry 2 million barrels per day 800 miles from the oil-rich North Slope to ice-free Valdez, Alaska, for tanker shipment to refineries. Above-ground construction would degrade scenery and, some ecologists fear, disturb the habitats and certain seasonal migration routes of Arctic fauna. Yet laying half of the pipeline underground, as current planning envisages, could cause even more serious disruptions. The pipe would cross areas of seismic activity, threatening a break. Friction between flowing oil and the pipe's interior would generate heat up to 140° F. Any melting of the surrounding tundra could loosen the pipe's foundation, perhaps causing the line to crack as underlying thawed earth settled beneath the oil's own weight. Opponents fear oil pouring from a rupture, ruining the ecosystem for years and miles about. With 11 thousand barrels of oil in each mile of line at capacity, even assuming perfect working of locks to seal off 15 mile sections in the event of accident, an efflux of 165 thousand barrels could occur.

Yet even this "maximum credible disaster" would effect a relatively small percentage of the Alaskan territory. Here too, localization applies, at least in relative terms. The project would directly preempt only one-hundredth of 1% of Alaska's 586 thousand square miles, albeit with severe local seral disturbance of an irreversible nature. The Interior Department's "Draft Environmental Impact Statement" (January 1971) stressed that construction would destroy arctic flora for 10 to 20 years even in minimally disturbed areas; delay reforestation from 10 to 150 years, depending on vegetative zone; prevent regrowth for a century wherever surface mats are removed to lay pipe or adjoining roadways; "irretrievably commit about 80 million cubic yards of sand, gravel, and crushed rock" at some unknowable cost in land degradation; and result in a heated "bulb" of thawed and muddy earth 20 to 30 feet in diameter along the line's underground portions.

For such damages, again, no meaningful dollar estimates seem possible—especially since pecuniary appraisals would have to be discounted to take into account the fact that the worst incidents (such as a massive break during an earthquake) might never occur. What does seem clear is that *approval of such a project implies a tacit commitment to "write-off" substantial acreage along the pipeline in terms of ecological quality as an additional cost of the facility itself.* Indeed, the same kind of implicit dedication of land as a "sink" for degradation might apply in reduced degree to the laying of new pipelines anywhere— even in less controversial projects through less pristine regions.

Of course, less spectacular failures already occur in the existing pipeline network. Offshore pipe leaks accounted for 27% of all pollutive spills in 1969 Coast Guard statistics, and for 113 episodes that year in which more than 100 barrels of oil were vented. Even more prominent in the public eye are hazards in the transport of natural gas. With gas, the danger is less that of environmental pollution than it is of explosions or leaks in populated areas.

Escaping gas is highly mobile. But the direct adverse consequences of a pipeline rupture are damage to property and, in some cases, to persons in the immediate vicinity. In 1969 there were 200 natural gas pipeline accidents (both intrastate and interstate) involving 15 fatalities and 157 injuries. Damage was reported in 63 of these accidents. For 43 of them, dollar estimates were given adding to about $2.2 million. Department of Transportation figures for 1970 record more than 5 times the prior year's number of leaks, an increase which doubtless reflects in part improved data-collection in this relatively new area of active Federal supervision. But again, the associated levels of bodily harm and property damage were comparatively low.

Table 4 sums up available information. These figures indicate that pipeline accidents occur with substantial frequency. But external costs—as measured in dollars—are not great in the case of either oil or gas. Even when lost resources are included, costs

TABLE 4

Pipeline Accidents, 1968–70 [a]

	Injuries/ Deaths	Damages (Thous $)	Number of Accidents
Natural Gas [b]	375/37	$5,157	1,219
Liquid Throughput			
Crude Oil	13/2	2,456	784
Gasoline	14/3	289	204
Liquified Propane Gas	29/15	934	115
Other	3/0	764	130
	216/80	$9,600	2,452

[a] *Source:* "Summary of Liquid Pipeline Accidents Reported on DOT Form 7000-1 from January 1 through December 31, 1968," Office of Pipeline Safety, February 28, 1969, February 13, 1970; Same Title, April 1, 1971; "Second Annual Report of the Secretary of Transportation on the Administration of the Natural Gas Pipeline Safety Act of 1968" and Appendix 1 of Third Annual Report.
[b] 1967 and 1970 only.

come to less than $10 million per year. This highly inflated figure is a small fraction of the total value of all oil and gas produced annually—and even of the internal costs sustained by the industry each year to increase public safety.

Summary: Pecuniary versus Ecological Costs

Although the original purpose of the energy industry's physical plant was to control fuel for profitable delivery in the market, the energy order might be given a more encompassing role. Because it offers a means of controlling a given throughput, *it may be the best mechanism for insuring that effluents are discharged across the economy-ecosystem interface in ways that maximize opportunities for natural uptake. The concentrative function of the energy order may complement the degradative and dispersive capacities of the natural environment.* With an improved, higher reliability network of couplings to keep energy resources concentrated and "in place," a given substance may be either kept fully segregated from the environment or released to the ecosystem for natural uptake at a rate, and in a location, controlled by the energy order.

Petroleum industry external costs till conversion probably go no higher than $158 million—allowing $28 million to cover offshore seeps, $120 million for spills, and $10 million for pipeline failures in a given year. These figures do not by themselves suggest true ecological costs—for example, seral disturbance of polluted aquatic ecosystems. They exclude damage estimates for deep-water oil pollution (i.e., from bilge pumping at sea) and for possible environmental catastrophes associated with projects such as the Alaskan pipeline. Nor do they cover depletive waste. True damage in all these categories may well be severe. Hence even overstated dollar estimates may, in the end, understate the true external costs of oil.

How is the discrepancy between oil's potential ecological harm and the apparently low pecuniary cost of petroleum's external diseconomies to be explained?

Under pressure from public opinion, and under the glare of publicity widely given to any embarrassing oil incidents, the petroleum industry has initiated extensive—and costly—environmental conservation programs. These attempts to internalize costs account for part of the answer. Moreover, oil-associated externalities during extraction and transportation are for the most part localized. The harm characteristically occurs where few persons are present or hold title to property (i.e., in coastal waters)—exactly the circumstances *where market forces are least likely to come into play, and hence pecuniary measures of environmental damage are most likely to diverge from a true ecological assessment.* The same factor underscores the need for some adjustment of energy policy, and a corresponding sensitization of energy policymakers, so preoccupation with conventional, pecuniary cost-benefit analysis can yield to a broader concern for non-pecuniarily measurable effects of energy production and consumption.

REFERENCES

The chapter epigraph comes from p. 386 of the Zimmermann book (1957). The oil evaporation estimate at p. 94 is based on experiments by P. J. Kinney, D. K. Button, and D. M. Schell, reported as Contribution 61, Proceedings, University of Alaska Institute of Marine Sciences. The brine-disposal problem, with statistics, is covered in the Interstate Oil Compact Commission's "Water Problems Associated With Oil Production in the United States" (Oklahoma City, n.d.).

Basic statistics are taken from "Crude Petroleum and Petroleum Products" reprinted from the 1969 *Minerals Yearbook,* and from the Interior Department *Mineral Industry Survey* (December 1970). The API-sponsored study referenced at p. 96 was conducted by Crossley S-D Surveys, New York City. It is available under the title "Report on Air and Water Conservation Expenditures of the Petroleum Industry" (August 1968).

The computations at p. 96 are based on statistics from National Petroleum Council, I *Environmental Conservation: The Oil and Gas Industries* (June 1971), esp. p. 36. The Mead-Sorenson Santa Barbara cost estimates appear in *Santa Barbara Oil Symposium* (December 16–18, 1970), University of California at Santa Barbara. Also used in connection with the Santa Barbara spill:

1. M. Foster *et al., The Santa Barbara Oil Spill,* Parts I and II, FWPCA Research Series DZR #15080 (November 1970);

2. Thomas A. Murphy, "Environmental Effects of Oil Pollution," Paper to American Society of Civil Engineers (July 18, 1970), Boston;

3. U.S. Geological Survey, *Environmental Impact Statement* (draft) on *Federal Oil and Gas Leases in Santa Barbara Channel* (May 10, 1971).

Gross tanker number, size, and spillage figures came from the November 8, 1970, *New York Times*. Coastal spillage estimates were furnished by the Coast Guard, as indicated in the Acknowledgments, and the data on off-shore oil venting and load-on-top deballasting came from Peter Hepple, ed., *Pollution Prevention* (1968), *passim*. See especially W. M. Kluss, "Prevention of Sea Pollution in Normal Tanker Operations," pp. 101 ff., from which the oceangoing biodegradation estimates were taken. Also useful in connection with oil spills are:

1. Department of Interior-Department of Transportation, *Oil Pollution: A Report to the President* (February 1968)—also used for basic pipeline statistics; and

2. API-FWPCA *Proceedings: Joint Conference on Prevention and Control of Oil Spills* (December 15–17, 1969), New York City.

The latter report is rich in information on oil spill effects, clean-up costs, and biodegradation and was used to supplement the Woods Hole material—again, see the Acknowledgments. The coastal spill estimates are taken from the report by K. E. Biglane of FWPCA and J. S. Darrier, U. S. Naval Facilities Engineering Command, in the conference report.

The Interior Department's "Draft Environmental Impact Statement for the Trans-Alaskan Pipeline" (January 1971) and *Questions and Answers*, a fact sheet from the Alyeska Pipeline Service Company, furnished basic data for the pipeline section.

Smog Shrouds New York City. The concentration of people and machines inefficiently burning fossil fuels, plus the difficulty of coupling the street level urban ecosystem to cleansing upper winds, makes any big city liable to severe air pollution. (Aero Service Corporation, Division of Litton Industries.)

Pollution increases not only because as people multiply the space available to each person becomes smaller, but also because the demands per person are continually increasing, so that each throws away more year by year. As the earth becomes more crowded, there is no longer an "away." One person's trash basket is another's living space. . . . as people live increasingly in city concentrations, their residues also concentrate there, and it is there that the problems become most acute.

NAS-NRC,
Waste Management and Control

6

Air Pollution in the "Urban Ecosystem"

The lone pioneer who set the pattern of America's fuel economy had no need to worry about waste disposal. He used some of his fireplace residues to make fertilizer and soap. The rest he carted some convenient distance from his cabin for free venting to the forest ecosystem. Gaseous effluents and light particulates went up the flue with lost heat, as the very physics of energy conversion performed an ostensibly free clean-up service.

Requirements for neighborly control of effluents set no limits on frontier behavior if there were no neighbors. Thus an imperative of waste *disposal*, as contrasted with mere waste *removal* for free venting and natural uptake, develops only when one person's inattention to clean-up will almost inevitably raise conflicts with his neighbors.

So, increasingly, is it today.

People packed into America's urban corridors and tied to a going economic structure cannot take the frontiersman's solution: "move away." So when the environment no longer absorbs pollutants, residues, and wastes, then pollutants, residues, and wastes become the environment. The choice then is to see the result of exploitation, and breathe it and drink it—or pay to remove it, prevent it, and clean it.

Coal and Sulfur Oxide Pollution

The Office of Science and Technology has estimated that electric power plants released 12 million tons of sulfur oxides in 1966. This figure is likely to triple by 1980 unless stringent new controls are enforced.

Current trends suggest a need for 500 steam-electric plants with 500 megawatt capacities by 1990. Only a fraction of these plants can be driven by nuclear power. Yet just one such coal-fired plant, if uncontrolled, will vent some 230 tons of sulfur dioxide daily. Depending on smokestack height, 50 tons can produce a 0.3 ppm concentration near ground levels over the adjacent ecosystem. Harm to crops starts at 0.3 to 0.5 ppm, and California standards consider 0.3 ppm over an eight-hour period adverse for animals too. Absorption of sulfur dioxide by water in the atmosphere creates sulfuric acid, magnifying irritant and corrosive effects.

Vented sulfur dioxide moves in the local air until intercepted by plant or animal. Such a situation shows a failure of the energy order to concentrate the effluent for control, perhaps even for commercial use. According to Lee DuBridge, a recent Presidential Science Advisor:

> If we took all the sulfur out of all the coal and all the oil that is being burned each year in this country and took the sulfur out of the stack gases, we would have a pile of sulfur

which exceeds the total annual sulfur production in the
United States.

There are three main lines of response. *First,* use high stacks.
Second, remove sulfur before burning, effectively raising the
ratio of low- to high-sulfur reserves by separating concentrations
of sulfur from concentrations of fuel. *Third*—also a concentrative
approach—remove sulfur after combustion but before discharge,
as in stack cleaners.

Assuming complete uptake of the effluent in the surrounding
ecosystem, the assimilative capacity of the metropolitan atmosphere depends on local conditions. These vary from inversion-
prone Los Angeles to the absorptive mixing layer of Minneapo-
lis-St. Paul. The mixing layer of relatively turbulent air extends
upward from building-top level to an inversion-cap or stratum
of stable air. A "deep" layer, in combination with stiff winds
aloft, most effectively disperses pollutants. With a shallow layer,
pollutants remain relatively concentrated as they rise and de-
scend in the turbulence below the cap.

Shallow mixing layers can be penetrated by high smokestacks.
These often discharge long plumes, sometimes extending for
miles, into the upper air for transport from the local area. Such
a plume is perhaps the telltale of impending pollution elsewhere
when the dust settles; but it indicates that effluents are being
vented where the upper air maximizes chances of dispersion
away from the city. Tall chimneys thus seek to decouple the potential polluter from the potential victim. *Such devices extend
the energy order—literally extend the physical casing which
controls the flow of waste gases. The aim is to couple an endangered ecosystem* (near the plant) *with a second ecosystem* (the
upper air) *more capable of absorbing and dispersing the waste.*
Of course, precisely because the high stack technique does im-
plement a true strategy of dispersion, it reduces local concentrations by contributing to area or global pollution.

As for techniques which use a strategy of concentration, National Air Pollution Control Administration research suggests an
average abatement cost of about $1.25 per ton of coal, based on
an optimum mix of concentrative approaches ranging from $0.50
per ton for mechanical cleaning, to $1.50 for use of low-sulfur

coal or throwaway flue controls. Natural gas substitution costs about $2 per ton. Application of the $1.25 per ton average to current coal use in power plants gives an abatement figure of about $450 million yearly. Total costs in the year 2000 could range up to $1.4 billion, even assuming timely development of breeder reactors so nuclear fuel can bear an increasing share of the generation load.

Yet doubling or tripling these abatement cost estimates would still leave a figure substantially smaller than the national damage costs of sulfur dioxide pollution. Russell Train, Chairman of the President's Council on Environmental Quality, has set $8 billion as a rough approximation of the externalized price paid for sulfur oxide pollution. Allocation of this total to the fossil fuels is given in Table 5.

TABLE 5

Rough Estimate of Sulfur Oxide Pollution Costs

	Cost	% of Total
Coal (billions)	$4.8	60%
Oil	1.1	14
Gas	—	—
	$5.9	74%

Notably, natural gas is virtually sulfur-free, leaving coal, oil, and industrial processes to account for the bulk of this form of pollution.

Oil and Carbon Monoxide

Oil accounts for virtually all carbon monoxide (CO) pollution. According to 1969 Health, Education and Welfare Department statistics, some 300 pounds of CO are released by an uncontrolled automobile burning 132 gallons of gasoline (about 2 thousand miles at 15 miles to the gallon)—up to a ton for every driver each year. But since the market price of gasoline represents a small fraction of the cost of driving a car, wasted fuel is often unnoticed. Hence the economic incentive for efficient combustion is missing. If combustion went to completion—if gasoline consumption were chemically perfect in an automobile's cylinders—no CO would be produced. (A diesel reduces CO emissions to one-quarter of the figure for a passenger car with comparable fuel use, owing to the more nearly complete combustion in its high pressure cylinders.)

Increases in population, in metropolitan densities, and in numbers of vehicles—all socially concentrative factors—will doubtless increase start-and-stop driving. Such driving profiles tend to worsen localized CO emissions as combustion gets less efficient.

A modern car at 30 to 35 miles per hour has a 13:1 air-fuel ratio, compared with a 15:1 optimum for complete combustion. In idling or deceleration, the ratio often drops to 11:1; this decreases gas mileage and increases partially combusted products. Idling boosts CO emissions from cruising levels by almost 140%. Hence CO concentrations are most likely to occur in heavy or stalled traffic, when one driver breathes another's emissions.

Carbon monoxide will reach dangerous local concentrations whenever a high effluent rate combines with poor ventilation. The contaminant escapes from the energy order (the car's fuel conversion and exhaust systems) to a local ecosystem—the populous, street-level city—which is incapable of absorbing the effluent. Sometimes too, faulty mufflers or flooring—another kind of flaw in the energy order—vent CO to the car's interior. Then exposed organisms absorb the pollutant. Human blood hemoglobin has three hundred times the affinity for CO as for oxygen, so even small CO densities tend to get further concentrated as an organism incorporates it in preference to oxygen.

Carboxyhemoglobin decreases both mental and motor efficiency. Discernible physiological effects occur at 0.35% blood carboxyhemoglobin, the incorporation level corresponding to 1 ppm of CO in inhaled air. A pack-a-day cigarette smoker may average persistent 3.5% concentrations, and 50 ppm air will produce an equilibrium level of 8% carboxyhemoglobin. Mean year-long CO concentrations are in the neighborhood of 7.6 ppm for typical cities, often going as high as 25 ppm over a "bad" 24-hour period. Up to 50 ppm for extended periods have been measured on streets, and as high as 200 ppm in tunnels and garages.

The Environmental Protection Agency on April 30, 1970 announced tight national standards for CO—9 ppm as a maximum eight-hour concentration, to be achieved in all locales by 1975. Prior to this action, standards in the 30 ppm range prevailed in cities like New York and Los Angeles, about 150 times the natural "background" level of CO, which is generally below 0.2 ppm.

Assume, then, that a city dweller regularly breathes 10 ppm air during 16 hours of the day, and suffers concentrations of up to 25 ppm for the remaining eight hours' exposure to traffic and inner-city activities. Further assume only a 2% reduction in efficiency results. Then, taking $110 as the average construction, manufacturing, or sales worker's weekly economic value added, a per-worker increase in economic output of $2.20 a week, or $110 a year, might be gained in the absence of impairment of alertness, well-being, and effectiveness from such "moderate" carbon monoxide exposure. Losses extrapolated for the 3.3 million construction and 19.4 million manufacturing workers amount to $2.5 billion annually.

It is difficult to control the location of CO venting so the ecosystem's combined transport-sink capacities can disperse the waste. Ventilation must be effective in the immediate vicinity of the exhaust, where humans are most likely to be. Yet automobiles can hardly be equipped with high stacks to couple them with the windswept ecosystem above. Thus the tendency of CO to become localized because inadequate coupling mechanisms cannot carry it off poses the real challenge to abatement technology. (An alternative abatement technique does not seek to transport effluents to the more-than-adequate cleansing capacities of the upper winds, but still exemplifies the coupling principle: Since CO stems from incomplete combustion, some designers of abatement devices seek to couple the car's manifold exhaust to a new artificial ecosystem—a thermal reactor which burns up unconverted fuel as it leaves the cylinders. This afterburner, rather than the car's engine, is coupled to the street-level ecosystem, to which it exhausts the products of more nearly complete combustion.)

Total CO output can lie near 1.4 thousand tons per day in the dense center square mile of a city of one million. Dilution to 10 ppm—still fifty times the natural concentration—requires four

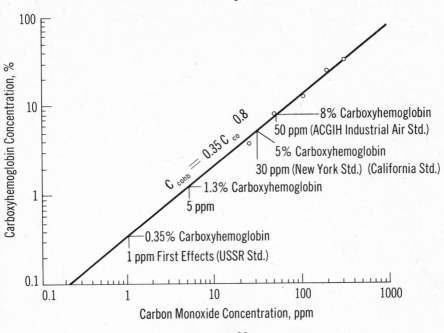

FIGURE 11

*Carboxyhemoglobin Concentration
versus Exposure to Carbon Monoxide*

Observable physiological effects start at an ambient CO concentration well below late 1960's and early 1970's standards. Allowable big city concentrations before EPA standards take effect would permit CO effects on the general population equal to that of pack-a-day cigarette smoking by every person. Adapted from Ralph I. Larsen, "Air Pollution from Motor Vehicles," 36 *Annals of the New York Academy of Science* (August 26, 1966), p. 284.

trillion cubic feet of air. In theory, this volume is obtainable if one-third mile per hour ventilating winds fully dilute the contaminants beneath an altitude of 1 thousand feet. In fact, recorded prevailing winds in American cities (measured for the most part at airports rather than in central areas) lie in the 10 mile per hour range—seemingly thirty times as much air as is needed to bring concentrations to the level at which they are often measured.

But nature's cleansing agents—the dispersive winds—are coarse in scale, unable to reach down into the canyons and pockets among city buildings. These winds, if made effective against local polluted air, should more than cleanse cities of CO, even at much higher rates of gasoline use than now occur. Again, however, *the problem is not one of inadequate environmental capacity to assimilate wastes. The problem is one of ecosystem coupling*—providing the means to carry CO from the local ecosystem a relatively short distance to an upper-air reservoir capable of rendering the contaminant harmless through dispersal and dilution.

In such a strategy—a true strategy of dispersion—moving air must transport contaminants away from regions of high localized CO concentration. But buildings, fences, and other urban structures interfere with blowing wind, converting its kinetic energy to turbulence. The air flow slows over a city. Eddies and vortices lose ability to carry pollutants away from the locale. Hence cities, where pollution is already self-compounding due to socially concentrative pressures, become natural sites for inverted air bowls with high contaminant concentrations.

As a result, specification of a single "safe" pollutant level—30 ppm, 10 ppm, or even lower—takes on a certain unreality unless it reflects awareness of a distribution of higher and lower concentrations. As shown in Fig. 12, even *after* strict standards become effective, the CO concentration in the immediate environment of drivers, pedestrians, and inner city workers might be multiplied by 5 to 10 or more over a prescribed "safe" average. And average dilution to 10 ppm might still imply that 40% of the city's air will have a 10 to 20 ppm CO concentration and another 10%, a concentration above 20 ppm. These estimates are consistent with the fact that CO in big cities actually is dispersed thirty times more slowly than would occur with unobstructed natural ventilation.

Hydrocarbons and Nitrogen Oxides

Fossil fuel conversion is the leading hydrocarbon source in populated areas. Discharge of this pollutant too is caused by in-

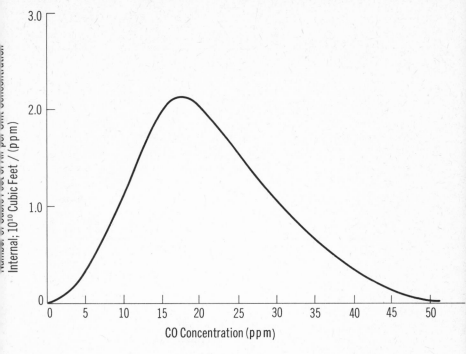

FIGURE 12

Illustration of Distribution of Carbon Monoxide Concentrations
for a City Air Volume of 10^{13} Cubic Feet at a Typical Average
Concentration of 15–20 Parts Per Million

The curve shows a typical pollutant-concentration distribution diagram for carbon monoxide in the air over a center city with dimensions 20 miles by 20 miles, with a 1 thousand foot mixing layer. At a given concentration measured along the horizontal axis, the height of the curve above that point gives the volume of air with CO concentrations in a one-unit interval about the concentration picked. The "average" CO concentration is 15 to 20 ppm, but there are air parcels with higher-than-average concentrations, such as at busy intersections. There are also air parcels with below-average CO concentrations—in the suburbs, for example, or high in the mixing layer.

The curve is a typical one. At a different time, or with different weather or traffic conditions, it could have a slightly different shape, subject to the requirement that the total area under the curve correspond to the complete air volume above the city.

complete combustion. In addition, evaporation of spilled oil couples the hydrospheric reservoir to the atmosphere. Then too, there is the evaporation from fuel tanks and carburetors of perhaps 15% of all gasoline marketed, *plus* some 775 trillion cubic feet of natural gas, mostly methane, vented or flared annually.

Chemical reaction couples these uncontrolled hydrocarbons to the nitrogen oxide cycle. Together hydrocarbons and nitrogen oxides account for 25% of air pollutants by weight. As with CO and hydrocarbons, nitrogen oxides over big cities exceed the natural atmospheric concentration, often by 1 to 2 orders of magnitude.

Yet there also exist instructive differences between nitrogen oxide and CO pollution. Maybe 100 thousand tons of nitrogen oxides per year will be vented from a center city of 1 million, 50% from stationary combustion, and another 39% from transportation. Using the dispersion model already employed to estimate a city's ability to cleanse itself of carbon monoxide, the vented nitrogen oxides, given average ventilating winds of 10 miles per hour, would dilute to a concentration of 0.04 ppm. Nitrogen oxides average for most large cities 0.03 to 0.06 ppm yearly, with peaks up to 0.8 ppm over shorter periods. These levels are in line with the theoretical prediction.

Is ecological coupling thus somehow twenty times as effective for nitrogen oxides as for carbon monoxide, since the same winds reduce the one contaminant seemingly much more effectively than they do the other?

The answer is Yes—but not because different principles apply in the nitrogen oxide case. Rather, nitrogen oxides are coupled to cleansing systems other than the dilutive winds. These have the effect of increasing nature's assimilative capacity.

Carbon monoxide persists in the atmosphere with a mean residence time of from 1 month to 5 years, according to a Public Health Service report. Thus CO will build to a high concentration unless dispersed by adequate air movement. By contrast, nitrogen oxides are liable to the scavenging effects of hydrocarbon combination and to precipitation in nitrate form, as well as to dispersion by winds and to biospheric incorporation. With all other things equal, the greater number of assimilative agencies will reduce nitrogen oxide concentrations well below the CO level.

Nitrogen dioxide produces free oxygen atoms. These bond to atmospheric oxygen, producing ozone, an attacker of rubber products. Unburned hydrocarbons react with this ozone as well as with ozone naturally held in the upper atmosphere—perhaps weakening the earth's protective shield against ultraviolet rays in the process. Hydrocarbon-ozone reactions then initiate chemical chains leading to smog.

Nitrogen oxides also carry through cycles harmful to man through direct somatic damage (by inhalation) and through environmental degradation (accelerated ecosystem aging from excess nitrogen fertilization).

A 0.05 ppm nitrogen oxide concentration is generally taken as acceptable—close to actually achieved concentrations in big cities, and about half the level at which physiological effects become noticeable. Yet lung deterioration is cumulative, so effects may go unperceived for years. About 85–95 percent of inhaled nitrogen oxides are retained, combining with water in the body to form nitric acid. Tissue turns leathery. As the lung's oxygen-exchanging alveoli are destroyed, the victim begins to experience emphysema. Statistics show an 18.3% increase in respiratory illness with persistent exposure to nitrogen oxide concentrations above 0.083 ppm.

Economists Lester Lave and Eugene Seskin have reported that a 50% reduction in all airborne contaminant categories would save society more than $2 billion annually, most of it in reduced respiratory-bronchial disease costs. This conclusion by no means covers all of the health categories affected by air pollution. Hence doubling the total estimate to $4 billion probably understates the true health costs of urban airborne effluents. Even if this imputed cost is equally divided among sulfur dioxide, particulates, and nitrogen oxides—thus understating the latter contaminant's known respiratory threat relative to other pollutants'—a $1.3 billion charge to nitrogen oxides results.

Nitrogen dioxide which neither combines with hydrocarbons nor is absorbed by an organism generally gets converted to nitrate. Lester Brown has estimated that nitrous oxide products of gasoline combustion in New Jersey add up to 20 pounds of nitrogen to the land each year, much of which eventually washes off into local waters.

The fertilizing value of such nitrate additions is not always an unqualified blessing. Ecologist Paul Ehrlich suggests that nitrogen deposited by rainfall from an automobile-polluted atmosphere has speeded the eutrophication of Lake Mendota in Wisconsin. Thus coupling of a polluted air-environment to an aquatic ecosystem—with precipitation serving as the transport medium—reconcentrates the nitrate right where it will do the most harm. Assimilation of nitrogen-rich effluents by an aquatic ecosystem then helps trigger a degradative sere.

Particulates: The "Dirt Costs" of Air Pollution

Particulates vented from fossil fuel combustion are subject to simultaneous (but partly competitive) processes—*dispersion* in the air, and lithospheric *assimilation* after they reach ground level.

Some particulates, such as the heavy salts from cars burning leaded gasoline, quickly fall to the ground. But rising drafts of heated air lift lighter particulates for atmospheric dilution. Some of these may remain airborne almost indefinitely, albeit with diminishing concentrations as air currents disperse them, eventually below the threshold where they threaten health. But as a persistent airborne haze they create other kinds of problems by reflecting off incoming sunlight, thus blocking the needed input of solar energy to the ecosystem. A 1969 staff study by Department of Health, Education and Welfare analysts estimated that $16 million annually are spent just for extra lighting to cut through air pollution.

In general, the larger the particle, and the lower its altitude at venting, the better are chances of its rapid return to earth through gravitational settling or precipitation. Hence particulate concentrations tend to diminish more than proportionally with distance from the smoke stack. Not only does the area covered (and hence the volume of diluting air) increase outward from the point of venting, but the weight of matter to be dispersed decreases as a result of heavier particles' more rapid settling.

This helps explain why reliance on a strategy of dispersion has not kept cities clean. *The environment's natural coupling and cleansing agencies cannot transport or dilute the larger, heavier particles.* These get quickly to ground level, where most of them undergo assimilation in the soil. *But some particulates inevitably are intercepted by persons, their clothing, machinery, or buildings.*

Inhalation of particulates is deleterious to health (by $1.3 billion or so each year on the basis of the Lave-Seskin analysis) and to cleanliness. Ironically, soilage is much easier to appraise in dollar terms than is illness. The existence of an active market for cleaning labor, soaps, and property maintenance services helps set an estimated soilage cost of air pollution much higher than that for disease—even though in most persons' value systems, loss of health or life represents a more serious deprivation than does wear-and-tear on buildings.

A national dollar estimate of yearly "dirt costs" from air pollution may be extrapolated from a study of "The Household Costs of Air Pollution in Connecticut" and a report for the U.S. Public Health Service on air pollution costs in the Upper Ohio River Valley.

By sampling household expenditures, researchers in the latter survey determined how often household cleaning and maintenance had to be done. In Steubenville, Ohio, drapes needed to be cleaned every five months. In Uniontown, with half the pollution, curtains and draperies needed cleaning only every nine months. In Fairfax City, Virginia, with half as much as Uniontown, cleaning was necessary only every fourteen months. In rural air, draperies need be cleaned only once every two years. An average figure was computed for how much *more* a typical urban dweller spends on cleaning and repair than would be necessary if he lived in "naturally" clean air. In the Ohio Valley, this increment averaged $400 per year per person—almost $70 million for the nine communities sampled, with costs increasing as a function of pollution.

In Fig. 13, twenty Connecticut communities' 1966–68 particulate concentration levels are plotted against the average extra per capita household cost of cleaning and maintenance. This plot gives a nearly straight line. Using the Connecticut cost fig-

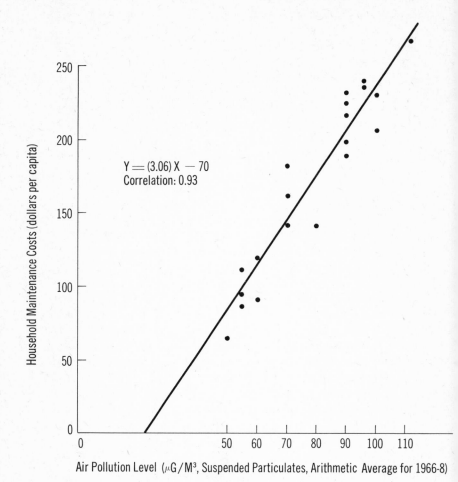

$$Y = (3.06) X - 70$$
Correlation: 0.93

Air Pollution Level (μG/M³, Suspended Particulates, Arithmetic Average for 1966-8)

FIGURE 13

Estimated Household Maintenance Costs Resulting from Air Pollution in Connecticut (20 Communities)

ures, it is possible to estimate a national total for particulate pollution. The bases of such an estimate appear in Table 6. Assuming roughly the same relationship between pollution and cleaning throughout the country as in the surveyed region, the Connecticut figures generalize to a $26 billion annual cost nationally.

Since the Connecticut study ignored extra maintenance for commercial establishments and public buildings, the $26 billion estimate doubtless understates actual soilage costs due to particulate pollution. On the other hand, and partially compensating for the understatement, this figure comes from an heroic extrapolation of limited data collected before environmental awareness brought control techniques to the fore. One can venture that annual costs of particulate venting do run to tens of billions. But $26 billion should not be thought a precise pecuniary estimate. It is rather a computational surrogate for a broader order-of-magnitude awareness.

About $5.65 billion in external costs may be attributed to coal, and the same to oil. This figure apportions appropriate fractions of the $26 billion total "dirt cost" to these fuels, and also includes a $1.3 billion annual charge for health impairment. It assigns transportation and fuel-burning 39% of the responsibility for total particulate pollution, in accordance with figures in the 1970 report of the Environmental Quality Council, and assumes that equal thermal units of coal and oil produce particulates in the ratio 3:2.

Next to these costs, the estimated price tag on controls seems small. According to the Secretary of Health, Education and Welfare's June 1969 report to Congress on clean-air programs, cumulative costs for control of particulate emissions in the 85 largest metropolitan areas, plus achievement of a variable level of sulfur oxide effluence, will range from $2.4 to $2.8 billion

TABLE 6

Costs of Particulate Pollution

Population Class	Number In Class (millions)	Particulates, Microgram/ Cubic Meter	Extra Cost Dollars per Capita	Extra Cost Total (billions)
Over 1 million	17.5	161	$420	$7.4
100 thousand–1 million	33.5	113	270	9.1
50–100 thousand	14.0	111	270	3.8
25–50 thousand	15.0	85	190	2.8
10–25 thousand	17.5	80	170	2.9
Under 10 thousand	81.9	—	—	—
				$26.0

through fiscal 1974. Setting the annual figure over four years at the higher level, and subtracting the cost of sulfur dioxide treatment, gives $250 million per year for particulate abatement.

Yet it is possible that even these relatively modest estimates are overstated. Particulate abatement costs would be reduced to their lowest possible levels if the widest range of suppression or prevention strategies were executed in an optimum mix, rather than relying on some single preferred technique on grounds of ease of administration and enforcement. Such an optimum "mixed strategy"—for particulates, and for air pollutants generally—would require constant variation in the local mix of techniques as effluent quantities, fuel demand, the ecosystem's assimilative capacity, and abatement technology change over time.

Harm from pollution itself can be reduced in three ways: (1) decreasing emissions; (2) increasing the assimilative contribution of the atmosphere by better coupling techniques; (3) providing artificial protection to the biosphere, such as issuing gas masks which will let air but not contaminants into the surfaces of interaction between the atmosphere and the biosphere. Much attention has been lavished on abatement, suppression, and dispersion, often at high cost. The third technique has hardly been studied at all. Yet, to cite but one example, many household air conditioners and filter units do in fact perform a decoupling function. Air comes through a conditioning unit by no means 100% clean. Yet filtration does perform a partial air quality service in millions of air-conditioned homes and commercial buildings. The contribution of such devices should be credited when appraising the total mix of pollution-control programs.

Summary: Toward a "Mixed Strategy"

In no area are localized degradative effects more pertinent analytically—or more serious in practical consequences—than in connection with air pollution. The severity of pollution is directly proportional to the effluent concentrations to which persons and structures are exposed. With other things equal, concentration is just as directly a function of the contaminants' localization.

Ideally, atmospheric ventilation would dilute pollutants, decreasing the probability that a harmful quantity of airborne wastes will come into contact with an organism. Such "ideal case" analyses have furnished much of the rationale for reliance, in the past, on a strategy of dispersion. But too often discharges are *not* distributed among potential diluting systems or sinks, as would occur if natural transport mechanisms carried effluents away from the receiving urban ecosystem. Pollutive build-ups result, with damages as estimated in Table 7, along with prevention and control costs.

TABLE 7

Fuel-Associated Air Pollution Costs—Billions

	Damages in Billions			Total Cost	
	Coal	Oil	Gas	Damage	Control
Sulfur Oxides	$4.0	$1.8	$0.1	$5.9	$0.450
Carbon Monoxide	0.2	2.3	—	2.5	0.400[a]
Hydrocarbons	0.1	0.3	0.1	0.5	0.028[b]
Nitrogen Oxides	0.3	0.8	0.2	1.3	0.072[b]
Particulates	5.6	5.7	—	11.3	0.250
	$10.2	$10.9	$0.4	$21.5	$1.200

[a] At $50 per car, with 80 million cars
[b] Control costs computed in proportion to damages

The estimates in Table 7 contain two types of understatement. The first type stems from a disposition to choose the more conservative number when making computations with such incomplete and inaccurate data. But even if all needed pecuniary data were available, true costs would be understated because the market has varying usefulness as an evaluative mechanism for different air pollution effects. So in a second type of understatement, health impairment appears to be less costly than other, *actually less serious* forms of harm for which pecuniary evaluations are more easily made. Thus, as with the ecological costs of oil considered in Chapter 5, *reliance on pecuniary evaluations can distort information because of fundamental inadequacies in the market, rather than merely as a result of practical difficulties in cost estimation.*

Another characteristic of energy use, like that of imperfections in the economic market, also begins to take on the nature of a general pattern. The environment as a whole has major unused capacity to absorb contaminants, including airborne effluents, if only these can be distributed quickly enough to an under-loaded sink. The policy implications of the ecosystem-economy interaction follow directly.

Most programs to prevent air pollution use a strategy of concentration: cleansing effluents so only "scrubbed" smoke is vented from smokestacks or tailpipes; removing contaminants from raw fuel through such concentrative processes as coal desulfurization. But the strategy of concentration is costly. It requires extensive human control. It increases the artificialization of the environment, for it extends the man-made energy order.

The alternative is to go ahead and vent effluents, while trying to take advantage of natural dispersive processes. If ways can be found to help nature dilute effluents, and provided no long-term pollutant accumulations occur, the strategy of dispersion is cheaper than the strategy of concentration, since the ecosystem does most of the work. But this strategy relies on, and therefore is hostage to, the effectiveness of the environment's own transport and assimilative capacities.

The challenge of air pollution is to find an optimum mix of concentrative and dilutive processes, rather than to maximize reliance on either the artificial energy order or natural dispersive mechanisms. Thus the energy order should not be viewed merely as a means of preventing emissions, or even of segregating wastes from the environment. At lower cost (and perhaps to equally satisfactory environmental effect), the energy order should be adjusted to complement nature's absorptive or dilutive capacities—using technology to "fine tune" the kind, amount, rate, and location of effluents ultimately vented for natural assimilation.

REFERENCES

The chapter epigraph is taken from the cited National Academy of Sciences-National Research Council study (1966), p. 3.

Generally useful data on air pollution are contained in *Air Pollu-*

tion, 1970 (in five parts, 1695 pp.), Hearings before the Subcommittee on Air and Water Pollution, U.S.S. (91st, 2d). The Public Health Service, Department of Health, Education and Welfare, has available studies of major air pollutants under the general title "Air Quality Criteria for . . .", with reports on sulfur oxides, CO, hydrocarbons, nitrogen oxides and particulates.

The sulfur oxide estimate at p. 114 comes from OST's *Electric Power and the Environment*, p. 3, and the DuBridge quote, from the January 13, 1970 *Washington Post*. The abatement cost estimates at pp. 115–116 appear in an address to the National Limestone Institute by Robert Hangebrauch and Paul Spaite of HEW, January 21–23, 1970. The Russell Train estimate at p. 116 comes from a White House speech on February 8, 1971, furnished by Terry Davies of the Environmental Quality Council staff. The percentage allocations to coal, oil, and gas of costs at p. 116 are based on data in p. 63 of the 1st *Annual Report of the Council on Environmental Quality* (August 1970). Also useful were:

1. F. E. Gartrell, "Monitoring of Sulfur Dioxide . . . The TVA Experience," paper for the 1965 American Power Conference;

2. Fred W. Thomas, "TVA's Air Quality Management Program," *Proceedings of the American Society of Civil Engineers* (March 1969);

3. G. O. Wessenauer, "Environmental Costs of Removing Ash, Sulfur and Heat from Power Station Effluents," paper for the FPC 50th Anniversary (June 3, 1970).

The basic CO statistics come from the 1969 HEW report, "Compilation of Air Pollution Emission Factors," plus the auto pollution studies by M. L. Brubacher and J. C. Raymond reported in the April 1969 *Journal of the Air Pollution Control Association*. The CO-associated dollar costs were estimated with data from Tables C-27 and C-30, 1971 *Economic Report of the President*. See also on CO pollution:

1. Brian Ketcham, *et al.*, of the New York City Bureau of Motor Vehicle Pollution Control, February 1, 1971, *New York Times*, p. 30;

2. Ralph Larson, "Air Pollution from Motor Vehicles," 36 *Annals of the New York Academy of Sciences* (August 26, 1966), 275;

3. John Middleton and Wayne Ott, *Air Pollution and Transportation* (1968);

4. "Reduction of Exhaust Pollutants . . . The New Jersey Repair Project," New Jersey Department of Environmental Protection, Trenton, New Jersey.

The respiratory disease increase percentage cited at p. 123 comes from the November 22, 1970, *New York Times*. The Lave-Seskin analysis appeared in the August 21, 1970 *Science,* and the New Jersey nitrous oxide estimate in Brown's article, September 1970 *Scientific American.*

The Ehrlich opinion on Lake Mendota is expressed on p. 189 of his book *Population, Resources, Environment* (1970), and the figures in Table 6 on particulate pollution by city size are taken from Vol. I of Arthur Stern, *Air Pollution* (1967), p. 84. The particulate pollution responsibility referenced at p. 127 accords with data on p. 63 of the cited EQC report (August, 1970). The study data cited at p. 125 were collected by Environmental Health and Safety Research Associates, New Rochelle, N. Y., and reported October 1, 1968 and February 9, 1968, respectively.

In addition, indispensable quantitative reference materials are:

1. *Air Pollution—Hearings Before the Subcommittee on Air and Water Pollution,* Committee on Public Works, U.S.S. 91st 2nd, 1970;

2. *Air Pollution and the Regulated Electric Power and Natural Gas Industries* (FPC Staff Report, September 1968);

3. American Chemical Society, *Cleaning Our Environment* (ACS, 1969);

4. "The Cost of Clean Air," Second Report of the Secretary of HEW (March 1970);

5. "A Study of Pollution—Air, a Staff Report to the Committee on Public Works, U.S.S.," 88th 1st (September 1963).

Technical data on ecological and meteorological aspects of emissions are in Syukuro Manabe, "Estimates of Future Change of Climate Due to Increase of Carbon Dioxide Concentration in Air," ESSA-GFDL at Princeton, paper for Williams College 1970 Summer Institute on Critical Environmental Problems; and Reginald E. Newell, "The Global Circulation of Atmospheric Pollutants," January 1971 *Scientific American.*

A series of articles in *Tellus,* volumes 8, 12, 19, and 21, provides generally excellent background on the issue of global atmospheric pollution, especially by carbon dioxide—the so-called greenhouse effect threat of temperature disturbance.

Two final major sources are the "Report of the Cornell Workshop on Energy and the Environment," February 22–26, 1972, available from Cornell and from the Legislative Reference Service, Library of Congress; and *The Economics of Clean Air: Report of the Administrator of the Environmental Protection Agency* (March 1971) —for the latest data on, respectively, the damages and the economic costs of air pollution. Finally, two volumes which anticipated, at least conceptually, much of the more recent work are Harold Wolozin, ed., *The Economics of Air Pollution* (1966), and Ronald Ridker, *The Economic Costs of Air Pollution* (1967).

Radioactivity Is Harmful to Living Things. A radioactive source, located in the center of a forest near Brookhaven National Laboratory, New York, gives experimenters data on radiation harm to organisms. Tree morbidity increases with closeness to the source. (Brookhaven National Laboratory.)

What seems certain is that there is some biological cost that cannot be escaped but must be "traded off" in exchange for the benefits of nuclear technology. Such trade-offs are implicit in the expansion of virtually every technology, not just nuclear technology. Excess deaths from cancer due to increases in ambient radiation have their non-nuclear analogs in excess deaths from emphysema due to air pollution.

John Harte *et al.*,
Patient Earth

7

Nuclear Power

The heat from fissioning a pound of U-235 (less than 1% of whole uranium) is stupefyingly large, with the ultimate thermal potential of 1.4 thousand tons of coal or 6 thousand barrels of oil. Because of nuclear power's dramatic promise to reduce reliance on depleting fossil fuels, this energy form is often viewed as a millennial new departure.

Yet from the ecological perspective, nuclear energy raises familiar issues: dangers of effluent concentration; the limited susceptibility of some wastes to purposeful control; the relevance of nature's dispersive forces when a resource—whether chemical or radioactive—escapes from the energy order. Technologically and perhaps economically, nuclear power represents a revolution. But ecologically it is rather an extrapolation of current patterns and problems.

Uranium: The Extractive Phase

Underground mines account for two-thirds of uranium recovery. This proportion is likely to increase as current operations deplete open pit mines, and as new deep deposits are located. About five hundred operations in eight states produce 6 million tons of ore annually, at 0.2% average grade—yielding about 4 pounds of "yellowcake" uranium oxide per ton of raw ore.

As stressed in Chapter 2, extraction also disorganizes the underground environment, making some energy-bearing ores virtually unrecoverable to future generations. If only 10% of energy-laden material in 0.2% ore is left behind, a year's domestic output would be associated with wasting some 1.2 thousand tons of yellowcake. Full recovery would reduce by 600 thousand tons the comparable grade ore needed to yield the same quantity of uranium oxide. At $15 per ton, the approximate value indicated for ore shipped in 1967, the cost involved comes to about $9 million.

Extraction also directly threatens miners through exposure to radon, a short half-life radioactive gas produced by uranium decay. Radon is present in all uranium mines. It is inhaled by miners, then decays, emitting energetic alpha particles which damage tissues as they penetrate the lung wall. The damage ultimately causes lung cancer mortality among uranium miners at seven times the rate expectable in the absence of radon exposure. In addition, uranium miners suffer all the safety hazards inherent in mining. Although the dollar burdens of disease and death represent relatively small sums, their severity varies directly with the fewness of the workers (and their families) who must bear the entire load—another case of inequitably distributed, "concentrated" externalities.

The third category of externality in uranium extraction—degradation of the land—also remains localized. New Mexico produces 54% of raw domestic uranium. Wyoming, Colorado, Utah, and Arizona account for another 36%. These states' stream systems are neither well developed nor extensive. So the erosive run-off and siltation problems associated with mine spoil have less relative impact in the western United States than they do in Appalachia.

But with the working of leaner and leaner ores, an ever higher percentage of materials must be discarded as waste at some point between mining and conversion. Typical uranium ores consist more than 95% of silicon and aluminum oxides —just plain rock, literally not worth the cost to carry to a special disposal point. Therefore mildly radioactive wastes from uranium processing pile up outside 16 mills in the mining states, adding a low level and relatively confined, but persistent, threat to bulk-waste disposal as an external cost of uranium.

These radioactive materials are liable to air- and water-borne transport—an undesirable ecological coupling which carries toxic substances to, rather than from, areas of higher population density. Wind easily picks up the powdery mill tailings. The radioactive dust then settles as the breeze loses its transport capacities on encountering the obstacles of buildings in nearby towns. Radiation in streams near uranium mills has been measured at twice the levels considered safe up to thirty miles from the plant. Operators attempting to prevent erosion by wind and water have seeded grass on waste piles, looking to reclamation by biospheric assimilation. Such projects have met with limited success. The uranium mill tailings inhibit plant growth—a phenomenon which parallels the difficulties of reclaiming acidic spoil heaps in Appalachia.

Because uranium ore is so lean by weight in usable energy, "consumption" of disturbed earth in the ore-processing plant is practically nil. Hence far more than with fossil fuel extraction, nuclear mining is a redistributive process: Earth is taken from its natural location and piled above-ground as waste. In the early 1960's, "bare" earth in western states averaged about $60 per acre. If the annual discard of, say, 5 million tons preempted only 500 thousand acres of this description, reducing its value by half, the cost of land preemption—even allowing no price increase since the early 1960's—would exceed $15 million yearly.

Radioactive Products: A Distributional Problem

Following milling to extract concentrated uranium oxide from newly mined ore, most nuclear fuel is converted into uranium hexafluoride. In this form, it is sent to be "enriched" by separating out some of the U-238 of which natural uranium mostly consists. This increases the percentage of U-235, on which a controlled chain reaction feeds.

These phases in the nuclear fuel cycle are shown as steps 1 to 3 in the schematic diagram of Fig. 14. Moving forward through input and burn-up in a reactor (step 4), to radioactive waste disposal (step 5) or recycling of unspent fuel following chemical reprocessing of reactor residues (steps 6–7), the fissile content of the material in general increases. And so, of course, does the radiation danger.

Thus, fuel rods ready for insertion into a reactor at stage 4 pose more of a hazard than do mine or mill wastes discarded at stage 1. The irradiated products of fuel burn-up are, in turn, more hazardous than in newly prepared fuel. The toxicity of reactor residues imposes stringent requirements for secure handling, either for disposal or for "reprocessing" to recover unspent uranium and plutonium created during the original fuel burn-up. Reprocessing thus represents an epicycle in the nuclear energy process whereby new or reusable fuel is concentrated by chemical means from used fuel, then cycled back for conversion. Yet reprocessing too produces waste products (step 8), and these are the most hazardous of all.

How much of which potentially harmful effluents should be controlled—kept within the energy order in concentrated form, raising the internal costs of nuclear generated electricity? On the other hand, *which effluents should be freely vented,* externalizing costs by submitting wastes to the ecosystem's absorptive capacities?

The basic response has been to put more reliance on control as one moves farther along the nuclear process, while venting some of the less toxic wastes in the early phases—extraction, milling, and conversion—directly to the environment. In the conversion phase, the main freely vented pollutants have been krypton-85 and gaseous tritium to the air, and aqueous tritium to the plant's outflowing cooling waters. Some krypton and tritium also escape the energy order during reprocessing.

Atomic Energy Commission estimates of krypton build-ups assume a 300 thousand megawatt free-world installed nuclear capacity in 1980. With continued uncontrolled venting, and

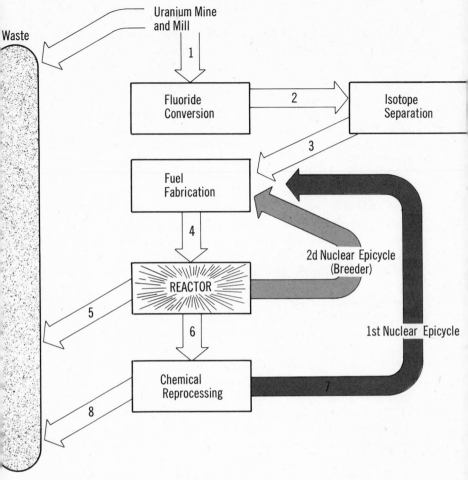

FIGURE 14

The Nuclear Fuel Cycle—and Its Epicycles

Wastes are discharged at three main points in the nuclear fuel cycle. Two epicycles reduce depletive waste—(1) *reprocessing* of spent fuels to concentrate still-usable fissile matter for recycling, and (2) *breeding*, whereby special reactors produce new plutonium fuel as they burn uranium. In 1970 the Federal government launched a high-priority program to develop a commercially workable breeder technology.

assuming complete dilution throughout the atmosphere, krypton-85 would contribute about 0.6 milliroentgens of exposure per year per capita to the world population in 1980, compared with an average natural background radiation of about 100 milliroentgens at sea level. Krypton-85's half-life is 10.76 years—long enough to permit a gradual build-up over time. As it builds, krypton-85 will increase the worldwide radioactivity dosage to about 2 milliroentgens per person in the year 2000, and to 50 by 2060.

Yet even this higher figure falls below the estimated average genetic dose from a diagnostic X-ray. It is less than a third of the allowable whole body exposure under 1970 Federal Radiation Council standards. And it is $\frac{1}{500}$ of the estimated minimum whole body dose needed to produce observable clinical effects in humans. To similar effect, continued free venting of tritium, followed by dilution throughout a 10 kilometer atmospheric envelope, in the circulating waters of the hydrosphere, and in the seas to a 40 meter depth, will lead to a tritium contribution of only 0.006 milliroentgens per year in 1980.

If freely vented effluents like krypton and tritium can be diluted to the levels envisioned in Atomic Energy Commission plans, then nuclear power under this heading promises a relatively healthier environment—so far as somatic effects are concerned—than would an entirely fossil-fueled economy at a similar scale of electric generation. Yet is is not clear that environmental dispersal will work so perfectly—or so uniformly, or so globally—as is sometimes assumed. Nor can one be confident that even dilute radioactivity will insure an equally safe environment from the genetic standpoint.

Like gaseous emissions from fossil fuel burning, radioactive effluents often concentrate, and in areas which increase the likelihood of exposure by living organisms. There are two main mechanisms of concentration: mechanical and trophic.

Mechanical Concentration. A Baltimore Gas and Electric nuclear plant planned for Calvert Cliffs on the Chesapeake Bay would discharge almost 3 thousand curies of liquid tritium each year. Tritium's half-life is 12.3 years. An equilibrium of about 100 thousand curies should eventually be reached, with new discharges just balancing the continuous tritium decay. But the effluent is liable to the same movement patterns that govern the water which transports it from the point of venting. For Calvert Cliffs, the diluting sink is the Bay itself—not the world's oceans. A particle injected to the Chesapeake is likely to remain 2.3 years before flushing out to sea.

New York's Lake Cayuga, on which 900 acres have been acquired to build an 830 megawatt nuclear plant, has a flush time of about 9 years. Thus vented tritium would tend to remain in this basin for almost one half-life before entering the connected circulating waters for more thorough dilution. For another example, some 7 thousand megawatts nuclear capacity are expected on Lake Michigan by 1973. With a flushing time for the lake of 30 to 75 years, a steady-state accumulation of about 7 million curies would exist by the year 2000. Thus mechanical forces—movement of the transport medium which couples the nuclear plant to its effluents' ultimate sink—concentrate radioactivity. Foreseeable concentration levels, however, generally lie below those at which safety would be menaced. For example, even the worst foreseen steady-state Lake Michigan concentration would be less than half of 1% of that allowed under the 1970 Federal standard. At projected 1880's levels of nuclear operation, mechanical concentration does localize hazardous radionuclides relative to the environment as a whole. But relative to the tolerance of human organisms to already existing variations in natural background radiation, the typical diluting volumes seem large enough to serve as sinks in which the substances can decay to harmlessness.

Trophic Concentration. A more compelling danger lies in the potential of trophic concentration. Concentration of vented radionuclides up the food chain might compound mechanical localizations which are safe enough by themselves. This danger seems not to apply to krypton and tritium. These are biologically inert, in that they have no tendency to incorporate in animal tissues. However, trophic concentration is a known threat for other species of radioactive products, especially those which are vented as isotopes or "twins" of elements vital to life.

Organisms readily exchange cesium—including vented radio-

active cesium—for potassium. Tissues eagerly incorporate stron-
tium-90 in place of calcium, so this mutagen has found its way
into childrens' bones through the nuclear fallout-grass-cow-milk
chain. Such trophic concentrations represent a form of ecological assimilation, but in the wrong direction. The highest biospheric levels—especially the omnivore, man—serve as the ultimate sinks.

In their proneness to concentration, such radionuclides
present an ecological anomaly. Environmental assimilation is
generally a disorganizing, dispersive process. Wastes are broken
down by human work, winds, ecological cycling, chains of
chemical reaction. All these agents of assimilation tend to decrease the localization of contaminants. By contrast, some radioactive wastes get increasingly localized—in the very guts of the
predators—as they move up the trophic levels. For instance,
White Oak Lake, Tennessee is used as a dilution pool for Oak
Ridge National Laboratory. In 1962, the concentrations of both
radioactive and non-radioactive cesium in bass exceeded that in
the water itself by a factor of 1 thousand. Radioactive zinc was
almost 9 thousand times as concentrated. Strontium, including
strontium-90, was 2 thousand times as densely concentrated in
the bones of bluegills as in the lake water. Studies in the Colum-
bia River below the Hanford reactors in Washington revealed
plankton with 150 ppm of radioactive phosphorus, caddis larvae
with 2 thousand ppm and minnows, 6 thousand—as much as
165 thousand times the surrounding water's concentration.

Concentration also has a potentially advantageous side. Localization of irradiated matter in one organism may reduce
other organisms' exposure to lower levels of the same radioactivity which would occur if the waste were dispersed through the
environment.

The Arctic lichen-caribou-Eskimo trophic chain has been a
notorious concentrator of radioactive fallout from weapons testing. This example has prompted suggestions that certain species
be used to suck up radioactivity, thus capitalizing on the fact
that concentrative processes inherently lend themselves to use as
control techniques. Edward Kormondy stated the case in his
popular text, *Concepts of Ecology:*

The high concentration ability of some organisms, some of which are in the order of tens of thousands of times above the environmental level, has led to a suggestion of employing such species to decontaminate a system. They could be introduced, allowed to concentrate the pollutant, and be periodically harvested and disposed of in some appropriate fashion.

Paralleling the concentrators of spilled oil discussed in Chapter 5, a radionuclide-incorporating organism itself functions as a little ecosystem. But a caribou contaminated by intake of radioactive materials is relatively weakly coupled to its surroundings. So although the animal takes in food, its radioactivity poses a minimal threat to nearby creatures. Harvesting of such "living vacuum cleaners," followed by special disposal, would prevent the natural death of the scavenger and its recoupling to the larger environment, since decomposition of the carcass would reinject the radioactivity to the ecosystem by admitting radionuclides back into geochemical cycles.

At foreseeable levels of nuclear generation, free venting of incorporation-prone radionuclides would—by contrast with effluents like krypton and tritium—present a clear public health problem.

To the extent that persistent radioactive contaminants escape to the open ecosystem, the most highly incorporative elements of the biosphere will in effect be appropriated to the energy order. These will then have to be viewed willy-nilly as radioactivity-control devices. Or in an alternative conceptualization of the same function, they will have to be "written-off" as natural sinks, following the pattern by which cumulative ventings of mercury caused swordfish, a highly incorporative species, to be transformed into a living sewer system. (Once mercury-wasting industrial plants were coupled to the open ecosystem, the phenomenon of trophic concentration made it more and more probable that the main mercury scavengers might eventually have to be decoupled from human cycles. Thus swordfish have been withdrawn as a food source.)

Unless radioactive wastes are themselves strictly segregated from the environment, with increased nuclear generation, organisms found to be incorporative of radionuclides will have to be decoupled from the main spheres of human activity. The resulting denial, as a substitute for accepting high costs of artificial segregation, might represent a not inconsiderable externalized cost of nuclear power.

Nuclear Energy and "Genetic Death"

Even if dilution and segregation could be made highly (albeit not perfectly) effective as nuclear effluent control techniques, some commentators on national policy would halt the growth of this energy form so long as *any* radioactivity threat remained, regardless how minute. The resulting controversy over the acceptability of long-term exposure to low-level radioactivity centers on whether or not any "safe" level of radiation exists. It is increasingly accepted that the probability of genetic damage is a linear function of exposure to radiation. Hence every dose, however small, adds to the chance of harm. By this view, there may be an acceptable exposure threshold, but not a "safe" one.

In this respect, the nuclear hazard accentuates the dangers of subtle, persistent chemical pollutants such as nitrogen oxides and carbon monoxide—all of which cause damage below the threshold at which "warning signals" are activated. Against certain forms of environmental hazard the species has evolved protective sensors. Thus man is warned off from poisonous hydrogen sulfide by the rotten egg stench of decaying matter. But as microbiologist René Dubos has pointed out, man increasingly finds himself coupled to an environment containing substances which, though potentially lethal, fail to excite adequate warning:

> Almost everybody is aware of the dangers associated with overeating, lack of physical exercise, chain-cigarette smoking, excessive consumption of alcohol or drugs, or exposure to polluted environments. But few are the persons willing to make the individual efforts required to avoid these dangers. Furthermore, the consequences of environmental threats are

so often indirect and delayed that the public is hardly aware of them. Many effects of the environment become inscribed in the body and the mind without the affected person's realizing that he is being changed irreversibly by influences that do not enter his consciousness.

What are the likely costs of radiation exposure, not only to those who will live with the 1980's nuclear generation levels but to their progeny?

According to John Gofman and Arthur Tamplin of Lawrence Radiation Laboratory, if the average American actually received the 170 millirad 1970 Federally approved "maximum permissible dose" per year above background radiation, 32 thousand additional deaths from cancer and leukemia annually would result, plus 150 thousand to 1.5 million extra genetic deaths, plus a 5–50 percent increase in schizophrenia. Nobel laureate Joshua Lederberg of Stanford University has estimated the annual costs of radiation-induced genetic illness, again at the 1970 allowable dose, at $10 billion.

Table 8 shows Lederberg's assumptions. Lederberg reasons that annual pecuniary payments of about $80 billion for medical care suggest a much higher true value for the burden of ill-health, including illnesses not treated. Lederberg assumes this

TABLE 8

Dollar Costs of Genetic Harm from Radiation

	Factor Used in Lederberg Computation	Alternative Assumption
1. Total Yearly Cost of Illness in U.S. (Billions)	$200	$135
2. Percent of Illness Assumed Genetically Related	50%	35%
3. Assumed Radiation Increase from Nuclear Power (Rad/Yr)	0.1	0.01
4. Resulting Increase in Harmful Mutations	10%	1%
Items 1 × 2 × 4 (Billions)	$10	$0.475

value to be $200 billion, shown in line 1. In fact, expenditures in the United States for health care in fiscal 1967–68 were $53 billion. This expands (using the Lederberg 250% increase) to an estimate of $135 billion in true costs. Line 2 compares Lederberg's assumption that 50% of all ill-health is genetically related with a more conservative 35% assumption, which is still substantially larger than a 25% estimate given by Lederberg himself in other popular sources. Then line 3 in Table 8 contrasts Lederberg's assumption of a doubling of background radiation by nuclear power with a 0.01 man-rads per year nuclear industry-associated increase. The lower assumption in fact seems more realistic. To get this lower level of dosage as a population average would require a ten-fold multiplication of the 1969 emission level. Even assuming no advances in shielding, and no progress to an inherently "cleaner" nuclear fusion reactor, the higher one hundred-fold multiplication of the Lederberg calculation far outreaches any projections of nuclear industry growth in the foreseeable future.

Radiation is thought to account for one-tenth to one-fifth of "spontaneous" mutations. Taking the larger figure as a basis for calculation, line 4 suggests that the smaller dosage increase will yield a 1% rise in mutations rather than Lederberg's 10%. Multiplying the figures in lines 1, 2, and 4 of each column gives an enormous variation in probable costs of future radioactivity. The variation suggests that Lederberg's figures may be overstated by as much as $70 billion for current total health costs, by a factor of 0.4 for genetically related illness, and by a full order of magnitude for probable exposures resulting from nuclear power in the 1980's. These discrepancies lead to a reduction in his $10 billion total estimate to $0.475 billion, or from $50 per person per year to $2.40.

What is more important, and less widely understood, is that such expenditures at whatever level would only in a small minority of cases be needed to cover lethal or even near-lethal effects.

It may take centuries for a detrimental mutation initially affecting a small fraction of the population to enter the species' normal genetic inheritance. And long before this occurs, elimination of a mutant gene through evolutionary selection—a phenomenon technically known as "genetic death"—may prevent a detrimental mutation from affecting more than a few possessors over several generations.

Only a tiny fraction of each year's genetic deaths is in fact associated with an individual death. That fraction itself decreases constantly with advances in medical care. Theodosius Dobzhansky, the geneticist, estimates that each person carries 20 thousand genes. Any detrimental expression of a radiation-induced mutation in one of these cells, such as color-blindness or diabetes, will reduce—often in an infinitesimal way—the possessor's ability to produce offspring. Failure of enough possessors of the detrimental traits to reproduce over time will result in elimination of the mutant gene from the species. This elimination, and *not* death of the possessor, is what is meant by "genetic death."

Hence while mutations may increase linearly with even small dosage increases, genetically associated human deaths are likely to increase at a much lower rate. A $500 million annual figure therefore seems, if anything, to overstate eventual nuclear-associated costs (by way of genetic impairment) from 1980's generation levels.

Of course, the true costs of genetic harm are always deferred, and deferred farther into the future in proportion as the mutation itself diminishes in seriousness. During the period in which the full genetic costs of nuclear power would come due, the price of medical care is likely to increase. So is human ability to diagnose and treat diseases of this description. The real hazard of a radiation-contaminated atmosphere is liable to accurate appraisal only decades, maybe centuries, hence. Perhaps, then, analysis favors the relative safety of nuclear energy, primarily because the long-time frame in which genetic harm could spread offers an opportunity to develop protective medical technologies.

Risks of Nuclear Disaster

Some one hundred accident-free reactor-years of operation in commercial nuclear stations had been acquired to the early 1970's—hardly sufficient for empirically based probability estimates of failure rates. Such failure rates should lie in the range of, say, one chance in a million for a "major" disaster if plant investment and operation is to be economically justified, let alone justified in terms of safety. Yet on the basis of design data, certain assertions are possible about the more likely kinds of trouble.

The disaster hazard comes not from any danger that a reactor will explode. The fuel used is not the highly reactive, nearly pure fissile material needed in a bomb. Moreover, safety devices should shut down a runaway reactor, mainly by inserting control rods to capture neutrons whose bombardment of fissionable atoms creates the heat-generating chain reaction. Yet some dangers remain: circumvention of safeguards by a cunning genoci-

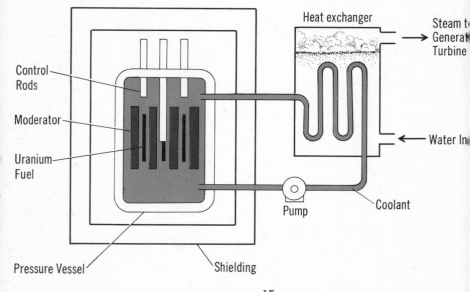

FIGURE 15

Schematic of a Nuclear Reactor

Burn-up of nuclear fuel offers an efficient means of generating heat to make the steam which drives an electric-generating turbine. Most of a reactor's complexity, and much of its design, goes into parts which moderate and control the burn-up and its radioactive products.

dal maniac; simultaneous compensating breakages of control
and containment systems which lead to a "nuclear excursion"; a
rupture in the energy order that leaks toxic wastes or irradiated
cooling fluids to the environment; catastrophe associated with a
natural disaster, especially an earthquake. All these contingencies are possible, though conjectural to the point of defying
meaningful statistical quantification.

Different in kind from such "technical failure" contingencies,
but no easier to quantify, are the political and military hazards
of the dispersion of nuclear materials. This problem gained in
urgency and in seriousness with the Atomic Energy Commission's espousal in 1970 of a vigorous program to develop the so-
called breeder reactor. As Fig. 14 suggests, the breeder would
add a second epicycle in the nuclear process, whereby even
more fuel is created in the reactor as a side-effect of U-235 consumption. Breeders have cores of fissionable U-235 or plutonium, surrounded by a "fertile" U-238 blanket. Neutrons released
in the core's fission reaction get absorbed by the U-238, producing still more plutonium. Thus in addition to heat, the chain reaction gives new fuel—indeed, more fissionable material than
the reactor consumes. Uranium in breeder reactors becomes a
capital asset that generates an income exceeding the principal.

Not only is the projected breeder's plutonium output eminently suitable for bomb construction, but the breeder reactor's
liquid sodium coolant is a highly reactive chemical substance.
Venting to the environment due to a flaw in circulation tubes or
in the breeder's pressurized containment vessel would have a
moderately explosive effect, inhibiting repair and increasing the
uncontrolled dispersion of highly irradiated wastes. Thus the
breeder program holds the prospect of substantially increased
external costs for political and military, as well as for improved
technical, monitoring of the nuclear industry.

Reactor failures have been rare, and improved design is
counted on to make them rarer. Only one accident has lead to
fatalities—at the Atomic Energy Commission's SL-1 in Idaho,
where three workers died in 1961. And only once has radiation
in large quantities escaped to the surrounding ecosystem: at
Windscale, England, in 1957. Compared to contingencies which
remain remotely possible, these were minor incidents. The Com-

mission's Brookhaven Study in 1957 calculated likely effects of a "worst possible disaster": more than 3 thousand killed, 45 thousand hurt, 150 square miles contaminated, $7 billion in property damage. The probability against such catastrophe for a given reactor in a given year was variously estimated at between 0.1 million and a billion to 1. Even if all improvements in nuclear planning in the years since 1957 are disregarded, and the Brookhaven dollar figure discounted by the mid-estimated probability of its occurrence, a trivially small "expected value" results.

Since the reactor failure probability presents an actuarial problem, insurance data perhaps give a clue to a reasonable annual charge for the disaster contingency. A typical new plant will carry about $600 million in insurance, both from commercial underwriters and under the Price-Anderson Act (71 Stat. 576). If 10% leverage is put on such guarantees—and the likelihood that full settlement would have to be made on any plant in a thirty-year amortization period is probably much less than 0.1—a $2 million fund would, in theory, have to be dedicated to "stand behind" a plant's insurance. For thirty plants in the 1970's, a maximum imputed charge of $60 million per year would result to insure against disaster.

Transportation and Storage: The Nuclear Energy Order

Reactors produce two kinds of waste whose toxicity exceeds the threshold at which free venting may be considered: low-level wastes (e.g., cleaning materials) and the much more hazardous high-level irradiated wastes. With the less dangerous residues, the main problems are acquisition of commercial space for disposal and economical transportation—both of which are subject to internalization in consumer prices—plus satisfactory public relations in a society increasingly preoccupied with any manner of environmental threat.

As the potential harm from misplaced resources increases, so does the need for physical integrity in the energy order. If enough is spent on safety systems, even the most toxic wastes can be transported within arbitrarily stringent limits of reliability. Yet hazardous shipments will continue to impose social overhead—extra costs, often unpredictable in nature, which cannot be fully internalized. An illustration might suggest the kind of problem that nuclear transport entails. John MacArthur of the New York Thruway Authority thus testified before the Joint Committee on Atomic Energy on July 20, 1966:

> We dropped a box in one of our facilities and a brown or sort of cream-colored liquid began to ooze out . . . We were tied up in a lot of ways. It turned out the box had the bad taste to land on top of a child's ice cream cone. I would not call that a radioactive materials incident. On the other hand, I wouldn't mind receiving, say $50,000 or $80,000 for the money it cost me finding out that it wasn't a radioactive materials incident.

High-level wastes from reactors and reprocessing need virtually perfect segregation *from* (as opposed to assimilation *by*) the environment. Since these wastes can be persistent as well as lethal, a strategy of dispersal is unacceptable. Trophic concentration can occur before the substance itself is degraded. Strontium-90 and cesium-137 have half-lives near 30 years. The half-life of man-made plutonium is 24 thousand years; of iodine-129, more than 17 million years. Some wastes (such as minute plutonium losses during reprocessing) require hundred of thousands of years' segregation.

Once again, there is no basis in experience for knowing whether any available container's useful life can be more than a fraction of the life of the toxic material it stores. Perhaps the pressure of growing nuclear waste volumes will not physically rupture the energy order. *But there is no guarantee that these wastes will not literally outlast the structure which must be built to contain them.*

In the April 1969 hearings before the Joint Committee on Atomic Energy, Milton Shaw, Director of the Atomic Energy Commission's Reactor Development and Technology Division, estimated that more than 75 million gallons of high level wastes were already stored. He projected an accumulation of another 3.5 million gallons by 1980, and up to 55 million by the year 2000. Such liquid wastes are kept underground in special tanks planned to last one hundred years or more. Nevertheless, fifteen known failures have occurred, eleven of them at Hanford, Washington. There some 140 thousand curies of cesium-137 leaked out and are decaying in soil about 10 feet below the tank bottoms. Fear centers on further seepage to connected ecosystems, as by an unexpected shift in ground waters.

The record suggests a need for better concentrative technology to improve controllability, and better storage facilities to insure permanent decoupling of ultimate disposal sites from the larger ecosystem.

Advancing solidification technology should permit concentration of the anticipated 1980 nuclear high-level waste accumulation to 35 thousand cubic feet, more than a ten-fold volume reduction. But the radiological hazard and heat per unit volume will increase with such compression, complicating disposal. The Atomic Energy Commission plans to bury these solidified waste cores, sealed in ceramic blocks, in mid-continental salt domes. Since salt domes are watertight, this plan would take radioactive refuse out of the "flowing state" characteristic of most natural dispersive processes.

Solidification, cooling of wastes for three to four years before burial, shipment, and storage in salt mines would cost about 20% more than "perpetual" liquid tank storage, and 0.5% per Kwh more than "free" venting of wastes to the environment. But such a surcharge would represent only the premium on an "insurance policy," not a guaranteed prevention of unforeseen damage.

Summary: An "Uncalculated Risk"

The persistence and subtlety of radioactive substances carries some risk—slight, but real—of causing long-term adverse genetic effects. At the other extreme, the costs of a sudden reactor disaster (e.g., an uncontrolled nuclear excursion due to an earthquake) or of a failure in high level waste-storage facilities would be equally beyond accurate pecuniary reckoning. But the odds weigh heavily against either cumulative or catastrophic harm—so far as can be determined on theoretical grounds.

"On theoretical grounds"—there lies the problem. *Decisions on whether to develop nuclear power to a scale where these dangers become credible must precede acquisition of empirical data needed to appraise the ultimate risks.* The Gofman-Tamplin charges, for example, clarified the subtle and cumulative nature of low-level radiation. A "latency period" intervenes between irradiation and activation of a malignancy. This delay may prevent the acquisition of data on harm from ambient radioactivity until years after policies have been decided which commit society, perhaps irrevocably, to self-damage. On June 14, 1971, the Atomic Energy Commission announced new radioactivity-release standards, tighter by a factor of 100 than had previously prevailed. This change represented a tribute to the cogency of the Gofman-Tamplin argument, just as it evidenced growing awareness of the uncertainties in the situation. Because of these uncertainties, the pecuniary externalities of nuclear fuel are, for the most part, only imperfectly calculable hedges against improbable future damages.

On the positive side, the margin of safety can be brought to an arbitrarily small level by suitable (though increasingly costly) investments in the energy order: better reactor shielding and containment; improved segregation-disposal technology to reduce free venting even of wastes like krypton and tritium.

Because of the huge thermal pay-off from even small quantities of nuclear fuel, relatively more can be spent to increase the integrity of the nuclear energy order (e.g., safety devices, reactor containers and shields, special waste disposal facilities) per unit of input fuel or output waste than with fossil fuels. In fact, nuclear development *has* been characterized by a general willingness to incorporate extra costs in price—even at the risk of making this energy form less competitive with other fuels, such as coal, whose histories have been marked by less attention to the externalities problem. Not all nuclear costs have been internalized. But most elements which are subject to meaningful pecuniary evaluation have been.

Nuclear energy already does go far to "pay for" its own share of an improved, high integrity energy order. Still, it cannot support the investment necessary to give perfect control, perfect safety, or perfect insurance against all future contingencies.

REFERENCES

The chapter epigraph is from John Harte, Robert Socolow, and Joseph N. Ginocchio, "Radiation," in *Patient Earth* (1971), p. 319; this article is a generally useful introduction. Other valuable sources on U.S. nuclear policy and possibilities are:

1. James Ramey, "Environment, Energy and Engineering," before the National Academy of Engineering, March 16, 1971, Washington, D.C.;

2. Glenn Seaborg, "Power, People and the Press," before the Associated Press Convention, November 19, 1970, Honolulu;

3. Philip Sporn, "Developments in Nuclear Power Economics," before the Joint Committee on Atomic Energy," December 21, 1969, Washington, D.C.

Statistical data on uranium miner safety appear in:

1. Federal Radiation Council, Staff Report #8, *Guidance for the Control of Radiation Hazards in Uranium Mining* (September 1967);

2. *Radiation Standards for Uranium Mining,* hearings before the Subcommittee on Research, Development and Radiation of the Joint Atomic Energy Committee (March 17–18, 1969).

The bare earth cost estimate at p. 137 is reported in a Federal Power Commission (Bureau of Power) memo dated October 24, 1962, made available by Chairman John Nassikas.

The AEC worldwide radioactivity estimates (both krypton and tritium) are taken from a July 23, 1969, presentation to the Joint Atomic Energy Committee of Congress, reprinted in "Selected Materials on the Environmental Effects of Producing Electric Power" (August 1969), p. 119. The projected 2000 and 2060 krypton doses comes from a study by J. R. Coleman and R. Liberace reported in the November 1966 *Radiological Health Data and Reports.* For tritium buildups in Lake Michigan and other waters, see "Environmental Tritium Contamination from Increasing Utilization of Nuclear Energy Sources," H. T. Peterson *et al.*, hearings, Joint Committee on Atomic Energy, 91st 1st.

The concentration statistics at p. 142 are from Sheldon Novick, *The Careless Atom* (1969), p. 97. The Kormondy quote comes from p. 193 of the cited volume (1969) and the Dubos quote from p. 156 of *So Human an Animal* (1968).

The Lederberg estimates are presented in the July 19, 1970, *Washington Post* and in an unpublished mimeo paper dated December 3, 1970, kindly furnished by the author. See, for much lower estimates of genetically caused illness, the Lederberg interview on "Genetics" in the 1971 *Readers' Digest Almanac.* The Dobzhansky reference at p. 147 comes from *Mankind Evolving* (1962), p. 146.

Physicist Ralph Lapp has published several popularized analyses of the nuclear disaster potential. See especially "Safety," *New Republic* (January 23, 1971), p. 18, and "The Four Big Fears About Nuclear Power," *New York Times Magazine* (February 7, 1971), p. 16. See also:

1. F. A. Farmer, "Reactor Siting—The Art of Compromise," before the American Nuclear Society, February 1965, Los Angeles;

2. G. K. Jones, "Cost Benefit Analyses of the Choice Between Nuclear and Other Fuels" (Operational Research Society, London, 1969);

3. Walter Jordan, "Nuclear Energy: Benefits versus Risks," *Physics Today* (May 1970), p. 32;

4. M. Phillips, "A Broader Approach to Benefits from Nuclear Power and Associated Social and Other Costs," 145 *Atom* (November 1968), p. 297;

5. Chauncey Starr, "Social Benefit versus Technological Risk," 165 *Science* (September 19, 1969), p. 1232.

Quantitative data on transport and disposal are drawn mainly from *Siting of Fuel Reprocessing Plants and Waste Management Facilities,* Oak Ridge National Laboratory Study ORNL-4451 (July 1970).

On the future nuclear energy context, see *Potential Nuclear Power Growth Patterns,* Systems Analysis Task Force, Division of Reactor Development and Technology, AEC (December 1970).

Also:

1. Atomic Energy Commission "Cost-Benefit Analysis of the U.S. Breeder Reactor Program," WASH 1126 (April 1969);

2. William C. Gough and Bernard Eastlund, "The Prospects of Fission Power," February 1971 *Scientific American;*

3. Glenn Seaborg and Justin Bloom, "Fast Breeder Reactors," November 1970 *Scientific American;*

4. Alvin Weinberg and R. Philip Hammond, "Limits to the Use of Energy," July–August 1970 *American Scientist.*

Wabash River Used as Natural Heat Sink. American Electric Power plant at Sullivan, Indiana, makes maximum use of ecosystem to dissipate waste heat from 400 megawatt unit. (Courtesy of the Indiana & Michigan Electric Company.)

Waste disposal is a productive use of water resources. To the degree that it is less costly than alternative courses of action when all offsite costs are considered, it *saves* resources and permits higher levels of production and consumption than would be possible if this resource use were prohibited or highly restricted.

Allen Kneese,
Economics of Regional Water Quality Management

8

Water Quality

~~~~~~~~~~~~~~~~~~~~~~~~~~~~~~~~~~~~~

The prime peaceful use envisioned for atomic energy is the generation of electricity. Hence most nuclear external costs may be charged to electric power. Fossil fueled electric generation also contributes significantly to air pollution. In addition, power generation poses a substantial threat to water quality. Two kinds of externalized adverse impact merit discussion: disturbance of riverine ecosystems by hydroelectric dams; and thermal pollution of water used to cool steam-electric stations.

Hydropower: The "Extractive Phase"

Mining of coal or pumping of oil extracts raw potential energy in the form of (chemically) stored heat. A hydroelectric project "extracts" the (mechanical) energy of falling water, converting it through water-turned turbines into electric power for distribution.

The costs of developing a hydro site go into the electric rate base. Hence they are internalized in the price paid by customers. Yet substantial externalities also occur, some of them beneficial. Hydro projects have turned indifferent streams into first rate reservoir fisheries (Red River-Denison Dam, for instance), or have created trout fisheries where none existed before (Hoover Dam in Nevada, Bull Shoals in Arkansas). Federal Power Commission licensing procedures require the developer to plan for scenic and recreational enhancement. Dams can help in both flood and sediment control—efforts which have proved notably successful on such rivers as the Arkansas and Missouri.

The energy economy's characteristic tendency toward localization of effects seems marked in these externalities. Electric power itself from a hydro project can be transported miles from the generation site. But such external benefits as scenic and recreational enhancement have geographical limits—the distance from the site which people may reasonably be expected to travel in order to enjoy them.

Adverse environmental effects are even more clearly localized. The main negative externality is reservoir siltation. The useful life of the impoundment behind a big dam in ploughed-over prairie land has been estimated at as low as fifty years. However, the newer, bigger projects have much longer time horizons. U.S. Army Corps of Engineers planning guides seek to reserve as much as 250 years' silt storage space in such developments. Nevertheless, at the site of every hydro project, some future generation must inevitably confront a mud flat of accumulated sediments, incapable of producing either electric power or recreation.

Ironically, flood control programs in watershed areas, which would take advantage of the soil's natural water-holding properties, are sometimes deemphasized after dam-building in the hope that hydro projects by themselves can handle floods. Meanwhile these same dams may be slowly clogged by siltation because of inadequate conservation upstream. Silt from the watershed upstream represents topsoil that is for centuries lost to agriculture. Overall in the United States, a typical river receives 2 acre feet of silt per square mile of watershed each year. America has already lost an estimated one-third of the average 9 inch cover which existed in the continent's pristine state—another form of deferred environmental cost, but one being paid right now due to the conservation failures of past generations.

A dam does not merely "change" the ecology of the river. It rather takes one natural system and creates two wholly new, smaller ecosystems—the lake above the dam and the down-stream river. The flow of water which drives the dam's generator turbines couples the lake to the downriver ecosystems. But the flow of sediments is too often decoupled as between the upstream river reach and the new reservoir (by the slow-down of water, which thus loses carrying capacity), and again between the reservoir and the river just below the dam. Because of these decouplings, sediments pile up.

Lakes may be dredged of accumulated silt, though not without harm to bottom life. Or secondary dams may be built upriver. Periodic releases of water in shock waves from these dams can sometimes carry sediments through the main dam's sluices. But such procedures are expensive. Desilting equipment for the Imperial Dam on the Colorado cost $1.5 million to handle only a fraction of the flow—the water diverted for irrigation to the All-American and Gila Gravity Canals. Most of this water has already been freed of silt by other dams upriver.

The external costs of hydropower do not end with siltation. Dams can adversely affect aquatic life. In the Pacific Northwest, elaborate and costly fish ladders had to be built so salmon could reach their spawning grounds. Dams have a recognized but intangible disaster potential, especially in earthquake country. An impoundment also reduces the water's ability to assimilate wastes. Therefore, in the lake behind a dam, any given level of respiratory activity will deplete relatively more of the available dissolved oxygen.

Siltation decreases lake depth, which increases the water's mean temperature, and brings the nutrient-rich bottom closer to the lighted and aerated upper waters. These changes cause both increased productivity and increased respiration. Eventually respiration may be limited by the rate of oxygen supply. Then unused production hastens the filling of the reservoir, which accelerates the changes that caused increased production in the first place. The eutrophication rate, which increases under anaerobic conditions, tends to speed the replacement of an aquatic system by a marsh-like ecosystem. The processes of siltation and deoxygenation thus become mutually accelerative, speeding eutrophication and emphasizing the inevitability of seral disturbance as an ecological cost of hydro power.

Water for Cooling: Supply and Demand

More than 80% of electricity comes from steam-electric plants, not from hydro projects. With hydro's share decreasing each year, moreover, the adverse ecological effects associated with "extraction" of electricity from flowing water are becoming relatively less costly. Countering this trend is an increasing thermal pollution threat from water used for central power station cooling.

Evaporation of water, which is thought to account for about 50% of all thermal transfer to the atmosphere, is a notably efficient heat dissipant, taking up about 1 thousand Btu's for every pound of water thus "consumed." Everyday 10% of the flowing fresh water in the United States is withdrawn for cooling purposes. Some 75% of the heat dissipated therewith comes from electric power plants—the most significant point-sources of waste heat, and by far the gravest potential thermal pollution threat.

Two factors portend a substantial worsening of the waste heat disposal problem. First is the projected growth in centrally generated power by all means—up to the 3 trillion Kwh range in 1980. Second is the expected relative increase in nuclear generation.

Heat dissipation requirements are higher for nuclear stations of current design than for fossil fueled plants by about 1 thousand Btu's more heat wasted per Kwh generated. A fossil plant's ability to vent perhaps one-third of its waste heat up a stack accounts for part of this discrepancy. Current-design nuclear plants are also operated at relatively inefficient levels to reduce fluid pressures. Steam in water-moderated nuclear plants is raised to only about 600°F. at 2250 pounds per square inch pressure, compared with 1050°F. and 3500 pounds in the best new coal-fired plants. The lower pressure reduces the danger of rupture in the reactor system's containment vessel. But a reduced steam temperature at the start of the thermodynamic cycle also lowers maximum attainable plant efficiency, which depends on the differential between the steam input and the engine's exhaust temperatures. More heat is therefore wasted. *Thus some thermal pollution from nuclear plants should be seen as a cost purposely sustained to reduce the risk of a more dangerous externality—failure of the energy order under too-high pressures, with consequent discharges to the environment.*

Since the nuclear frontier still lies largely ahead, developing technologies will be able to use more advanced materials and engine designs. Breeder reactors (using liquid sodium, which does not undergo the phase changes and consequent energy losses of the water-steam-water cycle) should operate at higher input temperatures, about equaling the efficiencies of the best fossil fuel plants. Thus with the breeder, nuclear generators in, say, the year 2000 might be more efficient than older vintage fossil-fueled plants.

But no projections suggest that nuclear's heat efficiency will improve apace with the increase in total nuclear output. The Water Resources Council in 1968 projected that cooling needs for coal- and oil-fired power will increase by a quarter or so between 1980 and 2000. Nuclear requirements will multiply by five. Thus more and more wasted heat will have to be dissipated in an environment whose assimilative capacities, some fear, are already overtaxed.

Such heat inputs can levy substantial demands on an ecosystem's ability to restore itself after the perturbation, or to resist major seral disturbance. Battelle Institute studies suggest that 25 to 35 hundred acres of pond water are affected for every 1 thousand megawatts generated by the plant whose waste heat must be carried off. On a stream—which is, in effect, a cooling pond in motion—some 8 to 12 miles of water may be heated before equilibrium is restored.

A study of nuclear power plant siting in southern United States indicates an average need for 7.5 thousand surface acres to return cooling water, after a 13° F. rise through a 2.4 thousand megawatt nuclear plant (at 60% load factor), to within 1° of the

ambient temperature. Some 4.2 thousand water acres are needed
to dissipate 75% of the waste heat. Taking 75% dissipation as a
rough standard for restoration of water to acceptable quality
gives a requirement of 1.3 thousand acres per thousand
megawatts—say 1.5 thousand acres. This is half the Battelle
figure of 3 thousand, since the remaining 50% of affected water
surface dissipates only 25% of the heat—the final, and presumably least harmful, increment rejected by the plant.

Bureau of Mines Information Circular 8384 may be used as
a rough guide to the mid-1970's thermal load. This document
projects a (probably low) input of 166 billion therms for power
generation from fossil and nuclear fuels—in about an 8:1 ratio
—in 1975. Of this input, 60% will be wasted, leaving a requirement for about 66 million surface areas of cooling water if all the
reject heat were to be dissipated in relatively still natural waters.

What would be the ecological effects of such a situation?

Thermal Pollution: Possible Ecological Effects

Even relatively small heat additions to natural waters can disproportionately affect the qualitative characteristics of an aquatic
system. The adverse effects of vented heat are not necessarily a
linear function of the input. Because of this non-linearity, a single undiscriminating temperature-rise standard should not be
applied simultaneously to systems in which a given heat increase has virtually no environmental inpact, and to others in
which the same input is likely to trigger an undesirable chain of
ecological effects.

One likely chain of thermal effects, occurring at the very base
of the trophic pyramid, suggests the pertinence of ecological
coupling to the variable capacities of different ecosystems to assimilate wastes—in this case, waste heat.

Small waterborne planktonic forms, called "diatoms" and
"green algae," provide food for aquatic life forms higher in the
trophic chain—protozoa and lower invertebrates, which in turn
are eaten by large insects, and on up through fish and men. Diatoms flourish in the 59° to 77°F. range, green algae at 77° to

95° F. These temperature bands are actually narrower than the ranges within which some of the higher, predator life forms can survive. Hence certain fish can be killed off by warming water to a point where diatoms and green algae die, even though the predators' own thermal tolerances may not be exceeded.

Blue-green algae or "cyanophyta," notorious sources of taste and odor degradation in polluted waters, survive in the diatoms' and green algae's preferred temperature ranges. They also thrive in hotter water. Therefore a heat influx from a power plant can kill diatoms and green algae, while encouraging the growth of blue-greens. Since the cyanophyta can continue to grow even in cooler water farther from the heat outfall, they are able to colonize neighboring ecosystems.

Blue-green algae are not in the food chains of most "desirable" higher forms. Therefore they proliferate in the absence of predators to control them. Blooming blue-green algae also make water turbid, blocking light and increasing the mortality of surviving diatoms. As algae die, their decomposition worsens oxygen depletion, decreasing water habitability for fish. Bacteria proliferate in the increasingly anaerobic conditions, metabolizing nitrates and releasing poisonous methane and hydrogen sulfide. Such degradation can cascade through a whole water body —*a major seral disturbance tripped off by initially minor changes in the ecosystem's species distribution. The vented heat itself remains localized. But through a chain of ecosystem couplings the colonizing cyanophyta export the heat's adverse effects to neighboring systems.*

Chapters 3 and 4 argued that environmental assimilation of some effluents—such as chemical air pollutants or low-level radioactive wastes—presupposes adequate ecosystem coupling so injected substances can be dispersed from the receiving locale. In theory, heat too could be made harmless by dispersing it so no one aquatic system would suffer a perturbation large enough to start a degradative sere. But in practice, heat is difficult to pump for more than 3 to 5 miles, even at substantial cost. Therefore, heat has an inherent tendency to remain relatively concentrated near its point of wastage. So it might be preferable to

permit localized heat intensification, *unless* free venting would
cause deteriorative changes cascading through neighboring ecosystems too. Even then, the easiest way to check such a spread
might not be by eliminating the effluent but by decoupling adjacent ecosystems so the disturbing factor is localized.

As indicated in Chapter 4, in Appalachia many small creeks
have simply been "written off" as sinks for acid flows, thus lowering the market price of coal by eliminating the cost of drainage treatment before mine water hits the receiving ecosystem. A
similar willingness to dedicate some aquatic ecosystems as sinks
for waste heat, even knowing that localized degradation will result, might be a fair increment to add to the true cost of
electricity—and a cheaper one than reliance on an extended energy order in the form of more artificial cooling devices to control dissipating heat. In a word, it may be preferable in some
areas to keep waste heat *localized* than to try to keep it minimized.

Technology might be developed to give heat plumes which do
not block an entire river flow, thus reducing the impact of the
thermal discharge on water downstream and permitting fish to
swim around the plume. Booms may obstruct the flow of noxious
flora and fauna outside the ecosystem affected by localized heat,
while permitting the stream's water itself to flow on—a partial
decoupling aimed at preventing adverse linkages between
neighboring systems. As a variant technique of partial ecosystem
decoupling, selective breeding of a biological scavenger for cyanophyta might be possible. *Where the links coupling a degraded ecosystem near a heat outfall to neighboring ecosystems
can thus be cut, there appear less compelling reasons to deny
power plants the use of nature's assimilative capacities.*

In the same vein, the criterion for allowable quantities of heat
rejection should itself be embedded in an ecological perspective
by relating it to the level of effluent likely to activate these
links. Research—indeed, a national survey—to support appraisals of different water bodies for these purposes is needed. The
temperature change which leads to long-term seral disturbance
may vary substantially from the thermal differential which will,
say, kill certain fish species or—usually more to the point—
scare fish away from the outfall plume.

The Energy Order as a Control Device

It follows that cooling ponds and towers should not be viewed as alternatives to "once through" cooling and discharge of waste heat directly to natural waters. Natural and artificial dissipative mechanisms should rather be considered as complementary, with man-made cooling devices used mainly to control the degree of vented heat's adverse effects.

The power industry has brought the "peak-shaving" concept to a high level of sophistication. Utilities rely on the least economical generators to meet high points in demand, leaving more efficient plants in continuous operation for the base load. Similarly, special artificial ponds or cooling towers could be used to meet special needs above natural heat sinks' capacities—on hot days, for example, or at peak operating levels. The projected increasing scale of new generating plants might well justify the capital expense for such relatively smaller, "peak-shaving" artificial cooling devices, even though they might not be in constant service.

Special ponds or channels to provide evaporative surfaces separate from those of natural waters represent extensions of the energy order. Yet artificial ponds have high evaporative water losses. Ponds are also costly unless land is very cheap. Both are reasons why reliance on the artificial water body technique should not be unnecessarily extended.

Similarly with cooling towers. Evaporative towers too have adverse environmental effects. Land is preempted, though not as much as with cooling ponds. Resources are used in construction. Aesthetic or navigational problems can emerge. Massive structures of the sort shown in Fig. 16 often rise 500 to 600 feet above the natural landscape. A typical modern cooling tower can put 2 thousand tons of water into the atmosphere each hour, a consumptive use of water about twice as high as with once-through cooling by natural waters.

A 1969 Federal Power Commission waste heat disposal study estimated a base capital outlay for water cooling of $2 to $3 per kilowatt of capacity with fossil fuel, and $3 to $5 with nuclear,

FIGURE 16

Cooling Towers Dominate Landscape

Each tower at Tennessee Valley Authority's Paradise Steam Plant in Kentucky is 437 feet high, could hold a football field in its base, and can vent tons of water vapor per minute. (Courtesy of the Tennessee Valley Authority.)

for a 600 Mw plant cooled by water flowing into the condenser and back to the ecosystem. An artificial water impoundment adds $4 to $6 for fossil and $6 to $9 for nuclear. Capital costs jump with an evaporative cooling tower to $5 to $9 and $8 to $13 for fossil and nuclear, respectively. A "dry tower" recycles water internally, eliminating the venting of vapor to the atmosphere, but at an investment cost more than five times that for once-through cooling.

Such capital costs are rolled into a utility's rate base, as are cooling tower operating costs. Because internalized, these costs are passed on to the consumer. But only dry towers completely eliminate the externalized environmental costs of massive steam discharges. Does this elimination justify an approximate doubling of cooling investment costs to go from evaporative to dry towers? Does the elimination of undesired, but often localized, effects on natural waters justify doubling capital costs to go from once-through cooling to artificial ponds, or an even higher increase to go to wet towers?

These questions pose a clear trade-off: ecological versus pecuniary costs.

Any heat injection to an ecosystem causes some seral disturbance. Such venting increases the energy cycled through the system, a hallmark of ecosystem aging. Eutrophication of natural waters is normally counted a "cost," if only in aesthetic terms. Against this cost must be balanced the goods and services foregone if capital is diverted to extend the energy order, relieving the thermal burden on natural waters. How much seral disturbance will every dollar of capital save? And which is more valuable—the water quality or the money?

In *The Ecology of Waste Water Treatment*, H. A. Hawkes reports that within a critical temperature range for organisms—above the "no effect" threshold, yet below the lethal temperature—biological activity increases with ambient temperature. This speeds seral progression. In the laboratory, the increase may be by a factor of 2 or so with every additional $18°\,F$. However, much less extreme thermally induced seral accelerations are commonly noticed in nature, even with persistent provocation by local heat discharges. The reason for a wide discrepancy between ecosystem and laboratory speed-ups is pertinent. Of the many factors which influence ecosystem aging, the thermal condition is but one. Often heat is not the "pacing" or limiting factor. Even in cases where the thermal factor can be identified as of primary importance, the heat generated by respiration or "consumption" of water-borne human and chemical wastes often exceeds the local perturbation from a power plant. As a result, the impact of even a substantial increase in one factor, such as power plant waste heat rejection, is likely to be much less than would occur if that factor were working in isolation.

Hawkes suggests only a 20–30 percent increase in biological

oxidation rates for an 18°F. rise in natural waters. This estimate is consistent with computations based on German water quality control experience, where a 6% decrease in a river's self-cleansing ability with a 9°F. temperature increase was found. Bearing in mind, then, that *withdrawal of all waste heat from natural waterways would not necessarily improve water quality unless other effluents are similarly controlled,* some rough estimates are possible.

Every 1 thousand megawatts of capacity are potentially associated with waste heat capable of advancing the ecological succession of 1.5 thousand acres of water surface by about 3%. This assumes a 5°F. effective temperature increase in the affected water (not in the condenser itself), and thus probably overstates both the impact of the vented heat and the resulting net thermal differential for properly engineered new plants. Taking 66 million surface acres affected at the projected 1975 steam-electric level gives a slight seral acceleration over 7% of the nation's 149 thousand square miles of major lakes, rivers, and streams, plus coastal reaches and bays. (See the intercept with the vertical projecting plane of the solid line in Fig. 17.)

But, presumably, some of the affected aquatic systems are already close enough to "turning points" in their ecological histories that even small quantitative increases in the rate of aging would produce major qualitative changes. The dashed line in Fig. 17 shows one possibility, corresponding to a 3% increase in the rate of eutrophication over 50 million acres, plus an 80% seral acceleration over another 50 million (15 from the thermally affected acreage, plus 35 million acres seriously degraded as eutrophication spreads through coupled systems). This gives 100 million acres of water brought to a weighted average 42% acceleration in aging.

At 9.3 thousand Btu's needed to produce 1 Kwh of power, the 16.6 million billion Btu's projected for 1975 will generate about 1.8 trillion Kwh. If roughly the same ratio of capacity to output obtains in 1975 as existed in the late 1960's, this would correspond to 400 million kilowatts of steam-electric plant capacity. Suppose all the waste heat from these plants were dissipated by artificial ponds and wet cooling towers in a 1:4 ratio. These facilities would cost about $2.2 billion more than if once-through

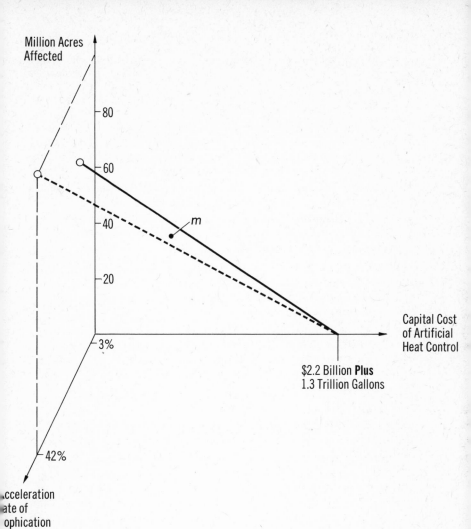

FIGURE 17
Pecuniary versus Ecological Costs of Heat Dissipation

169

cooling with natural waters were used throughout the utility system, a figure which includes the cost of up-grading plants operating before 1970.

In addition, annual evaporation would exceed that for once-through cooling by 1.3 trillion gallons—a notable ecological cost in itself, and one likely to limit reliance on artificial ponds and towers in areas with water shortages or fogging problems.

Adopting a mix of natural and artificial techniques (indicated by point m in Fig. 17, which assumes that the actual case in 1975 will lie between the solid and dashed lines as limits) would cost $1.1 billion for artificial cooling of about 50 billion wasted therms, leaving the remaining half of the total heat discharge to be absorbed by the ecosystem at a 23% average acceleration in eutrophication of 57% of the nation's waters. Coal would have to bear 67% and gas 17% of such an extra dollar cost at projected 1975 levels, $735 and $185 million, respectively. Nuclear power's share will probably exceed $126 million.

These figures assume that extensions of the energy order will preserve about 50 million acres of otherwise threatened water in the condition that would obtain absent central power station heat discharges. Roger Revelle, the Harvard water resources authority, has estimated $20 per acre-foot as the high average value of water in the United States. Then if the degradation prevented occurs near the water surface, where heat plumes can generally be engineered to lie, a weighted average retardation of 23% eutrophication over this area would have a dollar value of $230 million, assuming value to be an inverse linear function of the rate of aging. If even triple this estimate suggests the gain in water quality that a billion dollar investment will buy, then headlong rushes to expensive artificial cooling equipment may reflect a serious misallocation of resources.

Summary: Another Distributional Problem

Whether from hydro or from thermal generation, central-station electric power represents at least a moderate ecological threat to water quality.

The precise costs of hydropower are impossible to determine.

But it is clear that externalities in most major categories are sustained: depletive waste, as siltation threatens forever to deprive some future generations of an undisturbed waterflow, plus ecological aging and often pollutive build-ups as water impoundment reduces the assimilative capacity of the river. Perhaps hundreds of millions would be needed if capital equipment were installed to prevent these causes of ecological harm.

As with silt, the thermal problem stems from a "resource out of place." Thus one finds a recurrence of familiar patterns in the interaction of energy with the environment:

- The environment (including the atmosphere and space) has a major unused capacity to assimilate an energy-associated effluent—in this case, waste heat.

- But maldistribution of this potential resource threatens problems of local ecological degradation.

- Thermal pollution is best approached by adjusting the energy order to vent heat at assimilable locations and rates, thus *maximizing* the use of the environment's unfilled absorptive capacity, rather than by *minimizing* the total heat load created in responding to energy demand.

The most obvious means of thermal pollution control—reducing the total heat load to be dissipated—is the very alternative that increasing demand for electric power denies as a feasible solution. Reject heat *should* be cut back, but by improving conversion efficiency so more useful work can be realized from burning fuel, not as the most appropriate or economical response to thermal pollution.

In considering a deemphasis of artificial cooling structures, it is necessary to distinguish between accelerated eutrophication *within* an ecosystem's capacity to take up effluents, and degradation by thermal pollution *after* that point has been reached—especially cascading degradation through a series of coupled ecosystems. A lake or waterway typically has some capacity to absorb heat with little more than mild, local seral disturbance. If this capacity is not exceeded, vented heat need not seriously upset the ecosystem. Indeed, because it accelerates life processes, warmed water can actually be an advantage in irrigation and in "aquaculture" of oysters, shrimp, or fish. Therefore steps to increase the potential for constructive use of waste heat are preferable to "raw venting." Similarly, steps to increase nature's ability to absorb heat without harm beyond a localized area are preferable to dissipation through more costly artificial structures.

These propositions imply a graduation of uses—some heat channeled into aquaculture, desalinization, irrigation, and the like; the next increment discharged to natural waters up to the point where venting might cause degradation outside the localized aquatic region; and reliance on artificial mechanisms to dissipate heat that is unusable for constructive purposes or unassimilable in natural sinks.

REFERENCES

The chapter epigraph comes from p. 53 of the Kneese book (1964).

As indicated in the Acknowledgments, most statistical data in the hydro section were furnished by the Army Corps of Engineers. For the opposing view, and the fifty-year siltation figure cited at p. 158, see Elmer Peterson, *Big Dam Foolishness* (1954), p. 54. On the hydro project question, the following reports have also been used:

1. M. A. Churchill and W. R. Nichols, "Effects of Impoundments on Water Quality," reprinted from *Proceedings of National Symposium on Quality Standards for Natural Waters*, July 19–22, 1966, Ann Arbor;

2. FPC's *Recreation Opportunities at Hydroelectric Projects* (June 1969, U.S.G.P.O.)—a study rich in both descriptive and statistical information;

3. W. H. Peltier and E. B. Welch, "Factors Affecting Growth of Rooted Aquatic Plants in a Reservoir," 18 *Weed Science* (January 1970), 7;

Useful published sources on thermal effects include:

1. M. A. Churchill and T. A. Wojtalik, "Effects of Heated Discharges, The TVA Experience," *Nuclear News* (September 1969), 80;

2. R. T. Jaske *et al.*, "Heat Rejection Requirements of the United States," 66 *Chemical Engineering Progress* (November 1970), p. 17;

3. R. T. Jaske, "Use of Simulation in the Development of Regional Plans," before the American Society of Mechanical Engineers (June 1971).

The basic quantitative data on water effects come from a study by

William Lee of Duke Power Company of Charlotte, N.C.—referred to at pp. 161–162; the Water Resources Council's *The Nation's Water Resources* (1968); FPC's Staff Study, *Problems in Disposal of Waste Heat from Steam-Electric Plants* (1969)—made available by Mr. William Lindsey, FPC Bureau of Power; and Frank Parker and Peter Krenkel's *Thermal Pollution: Status of the Art*, issued in December 1969 by the National Center for . . . Water Pollution Control, Vanderbilt University, Report #3. The electric power growth projection of p. 160 comes from the draft 1971 FPC update of the *National Power Survey*, furnished by Dr. Haskell Wald, FPC Chief Economist.

The Battelle Institute study cited on p. 161 was reported in the September 1969 *Nuclear News*, and the William Lee study in the Joint Atomic Energy Committee's "Environmental Effects of Producing Electric Power" (February 1970), p. 2420.

The Hawkes estimates of thermal effects come from the indicated volume (1963), Ch. 4. They are based on experimental and field work by I. S. Wilson. The German data (based on research by B. Boehnke) are reported in I *Advances in Water Pollution Research* (1967), and the Revelle estimate is from "Water," September 1963 *Scientific American*.

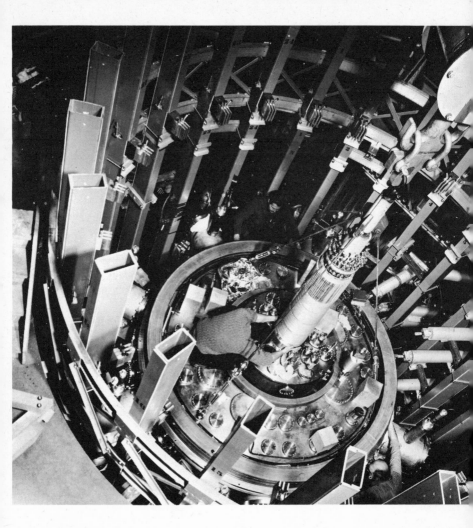

Basic Research to Expand the Technological Base. Workers at Princeton University Plasma Physics Laboratory, sponsored by the Atomic Energy Commission, install "FM-1" research device used to contain superheated hydrogen gas. Fusion of hydrogen nuclei under controlled conditions may yield virtually unlimited pollution-free power. (By permission, Plasma Physics Laboratory, Princeton University.)

If the nation is to have at its disposal a complex of energy resources that can meet constantly changeable needs and choices, the energy planning of the future must provide a dynamically balanced program that makes optimum use of the various energy resources, that maximizes the potential of this country's diverse R&D efforts at different levels of technological advancement.

Ali Bulent Cambel,
Energy R&D and National Progress

9

Improving the Energy Order: The Role of Technology

Environmental quality in a context of high energy demand can be neither free nor perfect. Even assimilation of effluents by nature produces some local degradation while the waste is undergoing dispersal or breakdown. Often a permanent change in the ecosystem as a result of seral disturbance will have occurred. Nevertheless, attention to the potential of the energy order as a fuel- and effluent-control device, coupled at innumerable points to nature's own supply and sink areas, suggests one path to a better environment at lower, properly distributed cost.

Pecuniarily Measurable Environmental Harm: A Real—but a Soluble—Problem

It was pointed out in Chapter 5 that the damage associated with pollutive build-ups, as contrasted with seral disturbance and depletive waste, are, in the main, most easily converted into dollars. Pollution, especially urban air pollution, generally occurs near population concentrations. Hence such episodes directly affect human activities. The value of such activities is characteristically set in a market—for example, the cost of labor to clean soiled buildings. Thus the market helps put a pecuniary value on the extent to which pollution impairs the working of everyday economic processes, as by necessitating more frequent cleaning in a dirty atmosphere.

Insofar as an overall dollar estimate is thus possible, at least in principle, it appears that *energy-associated environmental harm costs the nation tens of billions annually.*

Any more precise estimate is subject to wide variation, depending on the assumptions used in costing, the categories of externality included, and the accuracy of data in this patchy and woefully under-researched field. One such estimate is broken out in Table 9. It should be noted that the totals are reduced substantially by allowing for amortization of accumulated damages over five-year periods.

Air pollution accounts for almost 95% of the annualized $23 billion or so total in Table 9. Indeed, in dollar terms the probable margin of error in the air pollution estimate doubtless exceeds the combined values in all other cost categories. But this does not necessarily mean that pollutive forms of degradation are in fact most damaging or socially costly. It merely means that the other externalities tend to be understated, since they so often occur where markets function very imperfectly. Many coal-associated externalities are of this description. So are instances of oil blowouts or off-shore leaks. Such externalities can produce major seral disturbances of affected ecosystems—advancing the locale's ecological aging, or cutting back a sere with major kills of life-forms. But no mechanism is available to set a meaningful dollar cost on such effects.

TABLE 9

Pecuniary Externalities, Primary Fuels
(in Billions)

	Coal	Oil	Gas	Nuclear	Total
Extractive Phase	$0.8 [a]	0.028	—	0.024	$0.852
Transportation	—	0.124	0.006	—	0.130
Air Pollution	10.2	10.9	0.4	0.280[b]	21.780
Thermal Pollution	0.147	0.010	0.037	0.026	0.220 [c]
	$11.147	11.062	0.443	0.330	$22.982

[a] $4 billion from Chapter 2 annualized over a five-year amortization period.
[b] Reflects one-half estimated health damage from radioactivity (including "disaster discharges") at 1980–2000 levels.
[c] All thermal pollution figures from Chapter 8 annualized over a five-year amortization period.

Yet even after adjusting upwards somewhat, a resulting estimate in the $25 to $35 billion range per year is not so huge as to defy hope of improvement. *Energy-associated externalities present a real, though a soluble, problem.*

Table 10 gives figures on market price and consumption for the fossil fuels. These figures, again, are but the roughest of averages. Wide variations occur with different production and transportation costs from area to area, changing market demand, and external fiscal adjustments such as price controls (for instance, in the regulated natural gas industry) and oil import

TABLE 10

Fuel in America:
Projected Statistics—1975

	Cents per Therm[a]	Billion Therms[a]	Market Share
Coal[b]	4.1¢	169	24%
Oil	7.0	319	45
Gas	5.8	224	31

[a] Assumes 1¢ per therm price increase (production plus transportation) over 1969 level, at consumption in 1975 as projected in Bureau of Mines Information Circular 8384 (July 1968).
[b] Bituminous and lignite only.

quotas. Although the market prices paid by a hypothetical "typical" consumer can be only crudely estimated, they suggest that $23 billion for energy-associated environmental externalities would add in real terms about 3.2¢ to the weighted average cost of a therm of primary fossil fuel. This increment, which would raise by 54% a weighted average market price for fuel of 5.9¢ per therm in the mid-1970's, is both understated and overstated.

As already indicated, a pecuniary figure is inherently incapable of giving the full measure of ecological or long-deferred costs. Hence the dollar figure in Table 9 is likely to be understated. But the estimate is overstated too, since it charges fuel for the entire externalities burden. For example, the prime cause of air pollution is inefficiency in automobile engines. Therefore, allocation of due fractions of the cost of air pollution to inefficient machines and to social patterns (e.g., stop-and-go driving) would substantially cut the charge assigned to oil.

Moreover, the 54% incremental unit cost estimate neglects the growing rate of electric power generation. Even a large percentage increase in the cost of coal, oil, and gas used in such power generation would still end up as a small increment to the ultimate cost of electricity. In fact, about 36% of the $23 billion in Table 9 could fairly be assigned as external costs of electricity, rather than apportioned among the primary fuels. This 36%, about $8.4 billion, includes all nuclear and thermal pollution costs, plus 70% of other charges to coal and about one-third of other charges to gas.

Some 1.8 trillion Kwh of power are projected to be used in 1975, at about 2¢ per Kwh. Thus $8.4 billion if completely internalized would still account for only about one-fifth of the resulting unit price of electric power. The remaining costs of Table 9, added to the assumed mid-1970's fossil fuels prices, would represent about 32% of the resulting dollar cost of coal, 33% of oil, and 2% of natural gas.

Since nuclear is a "clean" primary fuel compared with coal and oil, the relative (and maybe even the absolute) environmental burden should decrease with anticipated changes in patterns of energy use. Even in the absence of further controls, then, the energy-associated externalities problem may be smaller than it appears. And demand trends suggest that it should get relatively better, not worse, over time.

But of course stringent new controls *are* already on the books, promulgated by the Environmental Protection Agency and aimed especially at air pollution. Control measures for air pollution generally occur at an extremely favorable benefit-cost ratio (see Table 7). Therefore any decrease in external costs should, in aggregate, more than offset increased prices for electricity, automobile engines, and gasoline—price hikes that will be required to cover anti-pollution improvements.

Altogether, these factors portend pecuniarily measurable energy-associated externalities in the mid-1970's which should add a moderate percentage rather than a multiple to the unit price of energy. That the externality issue thus seems to present a real problem, but not an earth-threatening crisis, points to the kind of adjustments in the existing energy order which promise reasonable progress toward a solution.

The Energy Order and Environmental Coupling

"Localization of effects" suggests a primary need to redistribute energy-associated externalities, not merely to reduce their magnitude. This indeed is the main lesson of environmental damage from coal mining considered in Chapter 4. *There exists in nature unused capacity to absorb ecological affronts of all sorts, if only wastes can be carried to areas whose "sinks" have not been used up, rather than being permitted to overwhelm ecosystems near points of discharge.* This is true of earth waste from mines. It is also true of urban air pollution. It is true too of thermal pollution, which would disappear if waste heat could be dissipated directly to its ultimate and infinite sink, outer space.

The needed redistribution can be accomplished in two ways: *pecuniarily,* by internalizing the costs of fuel production and conversion (including repair of environmental damage) so energy consumers bear the full burden, rather than persons who happen to be in the locale of the problem; and *ecologically,* by exercising better control over rates of effluent discharge and over the couplings between actually and potentially affected ecosystems, so full benefit can be taken of nature's assimilative capacities.

Since adequate coupling could disperse excess effluents to less burdened ecosystems, many costs of environmental quality should be seen as costs of transporting "resources out of place," either back to their original locations (as in backfilling mines to prevent subsidence, or in regrading soil for strip mine reclamation) or to points where natural assimilation becomes possible (as in dispersing spilled oil to facilitate natural biodegradation, or in redistributing silt by moving it downriver).

Nature itself furnishes the model for a system of dispersive coupling mechanisms—ecology's network of transport media such as blowing wind, flowing water, or even moving animals.

But high waste levels can over-tax the ability of these media to cleanse the receiving ecosystem. The response then is to extend nature's pattern by improving the artificial transport media which are already used to keep fuels in place—the nation's complex of rails, pipes, containers, and wires for moving energy that was defined in Chapter 5 as the "energy order." The energy order has long been used to couple productive sectors of the man-made energy economy to consuming sectors: coal mines to power stations via unitized trains, gas wells to home burners via pipelines, and so forth. The physical apparatus for transporting fuel may also be developed for the complementary function of controlling fuel-associates wastes. The energy order can then be used to couple some effluent-producers to natural sinks with the ability to "consume" them.

Urban air pollution, discussed in Chapter 6, illustrates:

- Effluents are injected to the atmosphere at up to thirty times the rates at which they can be dispersed to "safe" levels.

- Waste-producing systems cannot be *naturally* coupled to ecosystems where effective cleansing or assimilation could occur (e.g., the upper air, or geographically distant rural areas).

- To capitalize *artificially* on nature's assimilative capacities will require precipitators to concentrate large particles, high stacks to help diffuse gases and small particles, and controlling automotive wastes with thermal reactors to consume harmful wastes.

Implicit in an extension of the energy order to help disperse naturally assimilable wastes, would be provision for effective decoupling mechanisms too, in order to segregate wastes which cannot be thus assimilated.

As air pollution control illustrates the strategy of dispersal, nuclear waste disposal illustrates the strategy of concentration. Chapter 7 emphasized that nuclear energy intensifies the harm to be expected from any flaws in the energy order. Long-lived radioactivity out of place becomes dangerous at a lower threshold than do misplaced chemical air pollutants. Dispersion of high-level radioactivity would threaten ultimately greater damage than would undisciplined venting of most other contaminants. The needed segregation of nuclear wastes requires decoupling of the disposal site from its surroundings. Decoupling may also be achieved by prevention of emissions in the first place (as through flawless reactor shielding) or through prevention of radionuclide concentrations near life forms after venting (as by emitting only where no access to the trophic chains is possible).

Thus in the decoupling as in the coupling case, emphasis shifts from mere preoccupation with tonnages of effluents. The energy order focuses attention on the required characteristics of *linkages in the whole natural-artificial system* used to control wastes or emissions. Of course, these required characteristics will themselves vary with the level of waste output determined by such factors as energy demand and the current state of the art in abatement technology.

Depletive Waste and the Role of Technology

These prescriptions lean toward technological answers for immediate energy-associated environmental problems, while not necessarily denying the need for a long-term fundamental shift in American life-styles and values—away from "consumerism," high demand, and "growthmanship." Technology will also play a primary role in reducing depletive waste, which may ultimately pose a more serious long-term threat than either seral disturbance or localized pollutive build-ups. As was discussed in Chapter 2,

- Every 1 therm of usefully consumed heat is the output of a process which, on the average, results in the *irretrievable and useless waste of some 4.1 therms* of potential energy.

- There is substantial inter-fuel variation of depletive waste levels; *electric power is by far the most costly energy form;* among the primary fuels, coal is costliest, owing mainly to its lower extractive efficiency—even if wastage of human potential in accidents is excluded.

The cost estimate from Table 9 largely ignores accelerated resource depletion due to inefficiencies in current energy exploitation. The resulting "heat costs of heat" are likely to come due far in the future—as an externality passed on by present energy users to their descendants, who one day are likely to find themselves at the edge of the unused. In practice, no discounting technique reliably yields an accurate present dollar value of such long-deferred costs. Moreover, while the pecuniary externalities associated with the pollutive forms of degradation may get relatively smaller over time, the opposite seems portended for depletive waste. Thus, barring successful development of controlled thermonuclear fusion or of a safe, clean breeder reactor, projected growth in electric power demand threatens a more than proportional depletive pressure on primary fuels now in use.

At the same time, it needs emphasis that rapid spending of the fossil fuels does not necessarily deprive future societies of all options. A steep and positive technological gradient—that is, rapid technological advance to create new energy sources as old ones are depleted—can enrich future generations. With this technological gradient in view, the real issue of conservation policy becomes one of determining whether time's favors are tilted toward the present or the future. Is technology expanding fuel options more or less quickly than energy consumption uses them up?

Coal, oil, and gas are unrecycleable. But only if social-economic or technological trends conspire further to diminish society's energy *options,* rather than to offset options lost with diminishing fuel *stocks,* can a compelling case be made for stringent limits on the rate of use. Thus the aim of energy policy should not be to preserve physical reserves per se. The aim should be to maximize the options available to society over a reasonable number of generations, say, for the next century or so.

The rate of physical use—that is, of "using up"—of fuel resources is plainly sensitive to population level and living standards. More people demand more fuel, as do richer people. But depletive waste can also be viewed, at least in part, as a technological problem.

Technology can widen a society's range of options. First of all, there is a kind of leverage of technological efficiency, whereby improved extractive and conversion efficiency could help reduce the costs of producing wasted fuel as well as fuel which society actually puts to productive use. True energy costs depend on the entire stream of benefits and losses incurred from exploration for new fuel reserves to disposition of wastes after conversion. As combustion technology improves—and Chapter 2 emphasized the need for such improvement—less raw fuel is demanded to give the same usable heat output. Pollution is thereby cut too, since burning less fuel reduces the weight of exhausted residues. Following the process farther back, fewer miners or well hands would be maimed because relatively less coal or oil is needed. Today, as many miners lose arms or get black lung digging bituminous coal destined to be wasted due to inefficiencies in conversion, as they do producing fuel which eventually gives useful heat. Pipeline failures occur as easily delivering gas to an uninsulated house as in carrying fuel to an efficient boiler.

It is unrealistic to look for perfect efficiency. Yet by means of the leverage of technology, any substantial reduction in depletive waste through improved efficiency at any point in the process of fuel use tends to produce bonus savings in other external cost categories, from pollution to worker injury.

Archimedes is said to have boasted that he could move the earth from its orbit, given a long enough lever and a fulcrum on which to turn it. A wisely directed program of technological development can give policymakers not only the waste-saving leverage of improved efficiency but also a "fulcrum" on which to turn conservation policy. The fulcrum of policy is knowledge of the energy options that research and engineering may open up to future generations.

Like discovery of a new fuel form, breaking through existing technological constraints adds to future generations' store of usable energy. For instance, whenever improved extractive techniques increase commercially recoverable resources to offset quantities actually consumed, technological advance can leave society as well off as if both the advance and the depletion had not occurred. Again, suppose technology promised in the reasonably near future to provide a new energy source, such as controlled thermonuclear fusion. Then strict preservation of a current premium fuel, such as natural gas, could actually be anti-conservationist. Given a high probability that gas will shortly be supplanted as a source of heat energy by some new form such as fusion, such hoarding would deprive the present generation of valuable use-options—of clean air that could be attained if more gas were substituted for coal as boiler fuel—for no compensating benefit to the future. In this case, the optimum policy on use-rates of resources clearly turns on the rate and kind of technological change that can be foreseen.

On the other hand, suppose policymakers knew that no alternative clean, cheap energy form could become commercially feasible in the foreseeable future. Then precisely the opposite policy for natural gas would be indicated. Gas should rather be strictly husbanded for its most highly valued uses. Under the so-called premium-use theory, certain fuels may be reserved for specified uses as a matter of policy, rather than leaving their disposition altogether to free market allocation. Thus, pursuant to legislative act, fossil fuels might be reserved for use as petrochemical feedstocks, rather than permitting them to be burned for electric power generation. Or restrictions could be imposed to reduce the degradative effects of promiscuous resource use, such as undisciplined conversion of coal and oil for space heat, an "inferior use" which also adds to air pollution.

The social cost of depletive waste, then, depends on the overall efficiency with which energy is used—efficiency at the time of exploitation, relative to the efficiency achievable at a later time, when use of the fuel will have been denied by the earlier depletion. It follows that reduction of depletive waste does not necessarily require a decrease in the rate of fuel use, but it does require research and development at a level which stimulates technological advance at a more than offsetting pace. It is worth noting, finally, that stimulation of technological advance as a hedge against depletive waste is another variation on the redistributive theme. However, the redistribution occurs in *time*, rather than geographically or between economic groupings. The burden of a potential externality—namely, resource shortage— is lifted from some future generation and shifted forward in time. The using generation thus seeks to "fully defray" the cost of its depletion by funding programs to replace the options that energy use would otherwise deny.

Summary: Technology and the Ecosystem-Economy Interface

In an era marked by heightened awareness of the ecological dangers in industrial enterprise, an influential strain of environmental advocacy turns on arguments against "growthmanship." New life-styles and less materialistic national values are urged. Such changes would tend to cut demand for new products. If output got low enough, energy-associated effluents—and, indeed, effluents of all sorts—might then drop below the threshold of environmental harm. But as a short-run solution, such a strategy would probably cut jobs and living standards as well as pollution, to the extent that the social costs of halted economic growth might exceed the environmental gains.

Moreover, energy-associated environmental degradation is already below the threshold of nature's recuperative powers— except in identifiable, localized pockets such as big cities, mine areas, and oil-spill sites. So the immediate need is to redistribute energy-associated wastes, not necessarily to reduce production. This is not to deny any need for changed values. And changed behavior may indeed be a long-term requirement of environmental quality. Furthermore, generalizations which apply to America's energy economy may be irrelevant to nonenergy associated forms of degradation. Hence much more drastic

steps may be needed to control, say, municipal sewage or accumulating junk than seem indicated in the energy case. But
discernible improvement can be achieved in the near future, *so
far as energy's impact on the environment is concerned,* through
fairly straightforward adjustments in the industry's physical
plant and venting practices.

To some degree, technological fixes can rebalance the ledger
of gains and costs by redistributing energy's environmental burden. Assuming the desirability of a least-cost redistribution of
wastes, environmental policy should make fullest use both of incremental improvements in the existing capital plant and of nature's own assimilative capacities. *The first desideratum explains
the importance of an extended energy order. The second explains the importance of the ecosystem,* through which nature's
own contribution to waste disposal may be maximized. Thus the
energy order, originally developed to serve the consumer-ori-
ented energy economy, may be brought into a complementary
relationship with nature, whence fuels ultimately come and in
which most residues must ultimately be absorbed.

In this ecosystem-economy interface concept lies the case for
policies that support appropriate new waste-control technologies—as, indeed, has occurred in such fields as automotive and industrial air pollution, oil transport and spill cleanup,
and nuclear safety. Thus technological advance determines the
"tilt of time" by deciding whether development will insure the
increasing social wealth that can justify a rate of physical resource depletion favoring the present over the future.

Both technologically and ecologically, the facts of energy-associated environmental degradation support the viewpoint of
economist J. H. Dales:

> The taming of pollution problems is not really very difficult.
> It will cost a lot of money, but we are very rich, and we
> really don't want to "live off our capital"—especially our
> very important assets of air and water. All it requires is a
> resolve on our part to trade off a modest part of our goods-
> and-services standard of living for an improved en-
> vironment—and communication of this resolve to our
> politicians in no uncertain terms.

The real problem lies not in technological inadequacy or in the vulnerability of the ecosystem but in an incapacitated political structure which has delivered policymaking to manipulation (and veto) by special privileged groups. Fragmentation on the ecological plane into a series of localized ecosystems which are differentially affected by wastes is reflected in the image of American society as fragmented into a congeries of special interest groups. How this characteristic fragmentation inhibits policymaking—in the energy-environment as in other fields of public concern—is the subject of the following chapter.

REFERENCES

The chapter epigraph comes from p. *xix* of the cited study, prepared by the Federal Interdepartmental Energy Study Group (1964), directed by Ali Bulent Cambel. See also Tables 1 and 8, Bureau of Mines Information Circular No. 8384, for electric power projections underlying the allotment of externalities to electricity at p. 178. The Dales quote is from p. 108 of *Pollution, Property, and Price* (1968).

Toward a "Mixed Strategy" to Cut Air Pollution. At Metropolitan Edison's Portland, Pennsylvania, generating station, the stacks in the background collect and control effluents from coal combustion. Some wastes are disposed of; others are "recycled." Thus, sulfur dioxide is converted to industrial sulfuric acid, and piped to the tank car in the foreground to be carried off for marketing. (Courtesy of the Monsanto Company.)

It has been deemed the genius of American government that it was so constrained that it could not effectively govern—If we cannot alter ownership and control over production, the next best thing is to equip the government to ride herd on the uncontrolled forces of industry. It certainly is not so equipped now.

Duane Lockard,
The Perverted Priorities of American Politics

10

Eliminating the Negative

On February 26, 1972, an earthen dam across Buffalo Creek in Logan County, West Virginia, gave way under heavy rains. The dam had been built over the years from unstable coal mine spoil. A water impoundment 50 feet deep and nearly one-half mile long cascaded through Buffalo Creek hollow. More than 75 people died. Ten minutes after the flood passed, 5 thousand survivors were homeless.

The tragedy illustrated two salient features of energy-associated environmental externalities. First, the tragedy was *localized* in time and in place—another cost of coal displaced from society at large, and concentrated on hapless victims in Appalachia. Second, the tragedy was *preventable*.

U.S. Geological Survey studies of Logan County, West Virignia, had warned of unstable mine spoil dams throughout the area. The survey singled out Buffalo Creek dam in particular as liable to disturbance. (The Bureau of Mines denied responsibility for corrective action on the ground that while mine spoil lies within the Bureau's jurisdiction, dams do not!) U.S. Representative Kenneth Hechler, in whose former congressional district the tragedy occurred, had publicized the danger. The residents of Logan County had long known that any heavy rain could wash out the dam. Nevertheless, arrayed against their interest in safe environment were more powerful economic interests pressuring for coal production at the lowest possible dollar cost.

Soil stabilization or reclamation programs directed at mine-spoil dams would have added a substantial surcharge to the cost of producing coal. Given the already runaway market price of coal in the early 1970's, such a surcharge would have worsened this fuel's competitive position (versus oil, gas, and especially nuclear power) in the central electric generation market. The utilities, in turn, have every incentive to avoid petitioning state regulatory agencies for permission to increase their rates. Thus in the end, anticipated consumer pressures—the pressures to hold down market price—successfully resisted programs which might have prevented the tragedy at Buffalo Creek. Effective action had fallen casualty to a system of competing interests—a system that proved more effective in preventing than in initiating environmental regulation.

Nor are such cases unique to coal. Oil has perhaps the nation's most powerful lobbying interests, from oil-state senators to "the highway trust," from the directors of cartelized multi-national petroleum corporations to the gas station attendants whose prosperity depends on oil product sales. The electric power industry is a series of "natural monopolies"—with each utility a powerful, highly capitalized, regulated corporation giving sole service in a particular city, and developing a correspondingly magnified economic and political stake in that locale's public policy. The existence of such power blocks within the energy economy undercuts the classical assumptions of a "free" market. But since the market is not society's exclusive allocative mechanism—although it is the main one—imperfections in the economy need be left neither uncorrected nor uncorrectable.

The American *political* system is regarded as a sort of stand-by or fallback device, to make adjustments whenever the primary resource allocator fails. Through political action—such as redistributive taxation and subsidies—it is possible to relieve burdens that market imperfections would leave weighing on those groups least able to compete economically.

Yet in order for this stand-by system to correct rather than to intensify market imperfections, it is necessary that governmental institutions be in good repair. By the record of government action—or inaction—which culminated in the Buffalo Creek tragedy, this requirement is not met today. Nor has it been met for years. In the Depression of the 1930's, the nation faced an economic "crisis more serious than war"—the words of Supreme Court Justice Louis Brandeis. It took a "constitutional revolution" then to bring public authority into line with the continental scale of American industrial organization. A similar upheaval may be needed to furbish for action on the environmental front today's overlapping sub-Cabinet jurisdictions and jury-rigged layers of authority. What is the source of the current incapacity, and what may be done to improve the situation?

Public Interest versus Interested Publics

The estimates presented in Table 9 suggest that the dollar costs of energy-associated externalities are substantial, but by no means overwhelming. Moreover, proper use of the environment's own self-restorative capacities can moderate adverse ecological effects which cannot readily be appraised in dollar terms. And imaginative exploitation of technology, under the guidance of the energy order concept, can help achieve both a fairer distribution and a reduced level of environmental costs.

If externalities can thus be cut with reasonable environmental protection policies instituted at reasonable fuel price increases, why all the furor? Why does the environmental threat appear as large as it so frequently does, especially in the popular press and in "crusading" accounts of America's ecological crisis? The answer lies in the interplay between (1) the characteristic physical phenomenon termed "localization of effects" in Chapter 4; and (2) the parallel fragmentation of American society on the political-economic level into a congeries of competing special interests.

Given a willingness to accept a measure of accelerated ecological succession as a fair price for energy, externalization of some costs by dumping effluents into the surrounding ecosystem is not necessarily irrational. Nature *does* have certain absorptive capacities. It is sensible to use them.

But if effluents cannot be assimilated on the spot or be carried off to coupled ecosystems, they build up. The resulting costs of pollution may be small compared to, say, society's Gross National Product. But these costs are inequitably distributed. They develop only where a disproportion exists between local effluent loads on the environment and that ecosystem's assimilative capacities. Exploitable raw resources, the areas of greatest fuel use, and the discharge points for energy residues tend to be geographically concentrated. Thus severe localized harm can result near a coal mine, or in the locale of an oil tanker leak, or for residents of a city with polluted air.

Fragmentation of the environment into myriad smaller ecosystems, then, contributes to the localization of energy's adverse effects. This localization in turn contributes to an inequitable distribution of negative externalities. It is the inequity, and the consequent intensity of damage to those in the area of the overload, which makes headlines. This maldistribution of the burden shapes the popular view of environmental threats—and perhaps properly so!—although total damage may add only mills to unit energy costs when spread over an entire industry.

Fragmentation, leading to inequity, is not confined to the ecological plane. The pattern is paralleled on the political-economic level of American society. Again, the phenomenon originates in American history and culture.

Frontier individualism biased politics against innovations based on a spacious conception of a common "public interest." Laissez-faire saw material progress as resulting from untrammeled competition. Similarly, politics assumed continuing conflict among individuals and groups with competing—not to say hostile—interests. The late nineteenth-century ascendancy of Social Darwinism supported the notion that progress came from dog-eat-dog competition. Hence political scientists frequently refer to "group theories" or "pluralist models" of politics, in which government functions as an interest broker—that is, as an adjuster of competing claims by special publics.

The configuration of special "interested publics" tends to correspond to the distribution of environmental burdens throughout American society. Externalities are not mere random distortions in the market allocation of "goods" and "bads." Often externalities systematically transfer costs and benefits from one special public to another, or from society at large to specific privileged or victimized groups. Thus spill-over costs frequently fall not on those responsible—these often being the most resourceful or wealthy, and best able to defend themselves—but on those least able to bear or avoid the burden. Today's Appalachian poor, not yesterday's absentee coal magnates, pay the price of land despoliation in the hills of Pennsylvania and the hollows of West Virginia.

Government policy, focused on the "positive externalities" side of the energy picture, has traditionally reinforced such patterns of inequity under a system sometimes called, with grim humor, "socialism for the rich and free enterprise for the poor." American fiscal history chronicles a century of subsidies to those who are least in need of help, at least as measured by their economic and political power. In the main, the groups which benefit most from subsidies do so because they have economic and political—and hence lobbying—power. For example, oil import restrictions and depletion allowances have long benefited the petroleum industry. These externalities, fostered by government, positively compound the returns on exploitation of oil and gas resources. In both the coal and the petroleum cases, political forces are at work which reinforce preexisting economic and ecological patterns. Government sanctioned transfers of wealth help the rich get richer and the poor get poorer.

When externalities (both negative and positive) are thus patterned rather than random, they are most unjust—and potentially most vicious. They systematically over-reward some special publics. Just as systematically, they intensify the penalties paid by others for the accidents of their geographic location or regional histories.

Toward an Energy Policy: Political-Regulatory, Litigative, and Market Possibilities

The pattern of American political economy, then, parallels environmental fragmentation into a complex of local ecosystems. And interest broker politics has fostered an energy policy framework which positively reinforces both the fragmentation and the inequities. If a unified conception of the public interest is to inform energy policy, it will spring neither from the physical facts of ecosystem-economy interaction, nor from the modes of thought engendered by special interest-oriented politics. The large view will have to come from an impulse at the highest level to meet the challenge of energy policy as a single national problem.

The Political-Regulatory Crazy Quilt. The existing political-regulatory system can begin to redress inequities in the distribution of energy-associated externalities only if public power can be energized in the general welfare, over and against the demands of particular locales and interests. The existing fragmentation of governmental structure impedes coordinated policy-making. Worse, it tends to align public agencies with the special groupings in society. In this configuration, government becomes the veritable symbol of existing inequities, not a potential solution.

Basic energy regulatory responsibilities inhere in the fifty states' public service commissions. At the Federal level, creation in 1970 of the President's Council on Environmental Quality and the Environmental Protection Agency strengthened policy machinery at the national level in the environmental field. But these agencies' jurisdictions far transcend the energy-associated externalities area. Moreover, their creation further fragmented Federal authority in the energy field, already shared by—or rather, divided among—the Interior Department's Bureau of Mines and Office of Oil Imports; the Atomic Energy Commission; the Federal Power Commission; and the Department of Transportation, with Coast Guard cognizance over coastal oil spills, and Office of Pipeline Safety jurisdiction over appropriate aspects of oil and gas transmission.

The various agencies' actual jurisdictions are limited by statute, by personnel competence (which is highly variable, even from office to office within a department), and by the sizes of their staffs and budgets. Bureaucratic interests—and sometimes *conflicts* of such interests—also qualify regulatory effectiveness. The charge is often and rightly voiced that the Bureau of Mines, the Atomic Energy Commission, and the Federal Power Commission have obvious interests in the economic health of their client energy industries. Such a commission is not aptly situated to monitor its industry as a watchdog, rule-maker, and critic. Such patron-client relationships reinforce the fragmentation of economic interests. Government agencies become vehicles of interest brokerage on their clients' behalf, not moderators of competition in pursuit of a unified energy policy.

Specific responsibilities are also undertaken from time to time by Congress (e.g., in special investigations); by the General Accounting Office on instructions from Congress; and by particular high government officials in the executive branch—for instance, preemption of White House staff attention during the 1965 Northeast electric power failure, and again of the President's Science Advisor's time during the 1969 Santa Barbara blowout controversy. The Office of Emergency Planning, Executive Office of the President, played a major role in Federal planning for the Alaskan pipeline, urging that the North Slope oil field development was essential to national security.

Such fragmented authorities maximize bureaucratic competition, while minimizing chances for coherent policymaking.

Divided authority between the Atomic Energy Commission and the Federal Power Commission inhibits development of a unified policy for the supply and marketing of nuclear energy on one hand, and of fossil fuel-generated and hydroelectric power on the other. FPC has jurisdiction over field production and non-safety aspects of interstate transmission of natural gas, but not over retail distribution or marketing. Again, FPC has no authority over oil, although petroleum leaders have traditionally viewed natural gas as but a by-product of oil production. Regulation of domestic oil production falls largely to state public service commissions—or, in Texas, to the state railroad commission. These agencies effectively preempt Federal authority over natural gas to the extent that oil quotas—based in part on monthly Interior Department demand estimates—pace gas production from reservoirs rich in both petroleum forms. Meanwhile, the Bureau of Mines continues to function as the Federal agency with the primary direct impact on coal.

Proposals to consolidate appropriate Federal agencies into a unified Department of Natural Resources look to this end. So does the suggestion that the so-called Independent Regulatory Agencies be absorbed into the executive branch. These agencies are independent only of effective political control. They are *not* independent of their respective industries, and hence are of questionable regulatory value. Thus the Atomic Energy Commission and the Federal Power Commission would be taken into a single Cabinet-level agency, unifying fuel policy in unambiguous response to presidential direction through a single departmental secretary.

Short of such a major structural overhaul of energy-environment policymaking machinery—with a corresponding redrawing of congressional committee oversight responsibilities—governmental orgranization and practice will doubtless continue to reinforce the fragmentation of American politics into competing special interests. The political-regulatory system as now constituted offers little hope of policymaking in the national public interest. A patchwork of agencies that succumb to pressures from interested publics is even less apt to meet the challenge of negative externalities than is the market system, whose defects cause the problem.

What, then, of resorting to a second fallback system through increased reliance on the judicial process?

The Litigative Fallback: "We Will Sue and Sue!"   In a November 1969 *Fortune* article on electric utilities, the Conservation Director of the Sierra Club, Michael McCloskey, warned: "Our strategy is going to be sue and sue and sue." McCloskey foresaw a sustained effort to moderate growth in electric power generation. In the late 1960's, other ecological activists, sounding a similarly militant note, evidenced a similar determination to seek strict environmental controls through judicial decree. Courts would perforce become a prime participant in energy policymaking through the legal initiatives of conservationists.

Americans have traditionally put heavy reliance on judicial solution of disputes, often thinking the legal process "cleaner" or "fairer" than determination of public policy through political means. Broadly, two avenues of conflict resolution are available to those who, like Sierra Club opponents of industrial encroachment, seek legal protection.

The first avenue is the court system itself, activated by bringing a lawsuit or a criminal charge in a "trial court." A decision by this court may be appealed to higher tribunals. If the issues involved are deemed sufficiently important and far reaching in their impact on public policy, a case may be appealed by successive losers at intermediate levels of litigation all the way to the Supreme Court.

A second avenue of legal action has been opened up by the growth in the twentieth-century of administrative agencies at both Federal and state levels. Thus regulatory agencies have been set up to decide complex issues—for example, the rates at which "legal monopolies" such as electric utilities may sell electric power, thus preventing abuse of their privileged position. Regulatory agencies, functioning much as courts do by deciding specific cases brought before them by industry lawyers or spokesmen for consumer interests, are presumed to have special expertise within the areas of their jurisdiction. This expertise theoretically permits informed, expeditious disposition of issues that would enmesh a conventional court in problems beyond a "generalist judge's" competence, or a legislature in tedious detail.

By the early 1970's major decision processes—such as those bearing on the permissible extent of off-shore oil drilling along the Gulf Coast, on construction of the Alaskan pipeline and on allowable radioactivity emission standards for nuclear power generating stations—had been tied up in litigation.

Imperfections in the market should, in democratic theory, lead to corrective actions taken through the political system. Judicial review and litigative redress in areas of broad policy are ideally available only as auxiliary fallbacks when the political process has broken down, just as political correctives should need to be invoked only on failure of free and private decentralized decisionmaking in the market. The new reliance on the litigative process thus signals a kind of despair over the primary and secondary (that is, the economic and political) allocative systems. But such reliance is likely to prove misplaced. This is not to suggest that individual rights may fail in specific cases to find shelter in "the bosom of the law." But it is to suggest that the individual's gain on either side in such cases—whether that of the conservationist or of the industrialist accused of polluting —may be achieved at the expense of comprehensive national policymaking in the public interest.

The litigative process was simply not designed to produce the sort of long-range "public-interested" policy decisions that are called for in the area of energy's environmental impact. Procedurally, the legal process is cumbersome and conservative. It is inflexible and inefficient. Substantively, law cherishes the very values which a foresighted national policy in the energy-environment field may require to be compromised.

The frontier view of nature as an object of plunder—and that without defenses—biased American public law to protect just those attitudes that led to environmental depletion. Law offered an inducement to exploitation. For it offered security in the fruits of exploitation under nineteenth-century doctrines of the sanctity of private property. If values of untrammeled individualism were to be encouraged in the interest of a free and expanding economy, these same values certainly had to be legalized. Virtually all instances of depletive waste, seral disturbance, and environmental pollution stem from profligate enjoyment by a private individual of his property rights. Yet nineteenth-century American law, plus all its panoply and procedure, was constituted to secure the rights to that enjoyment. Much of the same bias has been retained in contemporary legal doctrine. Is this system either an appropriate or a potentially effective forum for reversing the trend of history?

Reliance on the judicial process seems the more extravagant in view of the unencouraging record to date of policy formulation by litigative techniques. Already to an inordinate degree, energy policy gets made at second hand. Commissioners (in Fed-

eral and state regulatory agencies) and judges reach their decisions in a process whose main purpose is to protect existing
vested rights, not to develop prudent long-range policy.

Each regulatory agency has statutory authorities over a specific sector of the economy. Each must make rules of general application. These powers are legislative in nature, but the process
is essentially judicial. On-going disputes between interested parties, not general policy problems anticipated from the
standpoint of the public interest, occasion the start of a regulatory case. The adversary technique is emphasized. Such a process, with issues polarized between disputants, is conducive neither to originality nor to the more spacious view that the public
interest requires.

An example of litigative policymaking would be helpful. In
1954 the Supreme Court gave the Federal Power Commission
jurisdiction over sales of natural gas at the well head, provided
the gas was intended for interstate commerce. Until 1961, these
gas prices were set in company-by-company hearings. Then the
"area rate concept" was adopted. Ceiling rates were to be fixed
for all gas recovered in a defined geographical area. By mid-
1967, two area rate hearings had been virtually completed, together covering some 43 percent of all gas sold in interstate
commerce. An internal FPC study found that $67.4 million could
have been saved consumers in lower fuel rates if just the first
(and by far the smaller) of the two hearings could have ended
with issuance of the Commissioners' rate-setting decision in half
the time that the case actually took: ". . . the true cost of [the
Permian area rate case]—directly through support of FPC in the
Federal budget, and indirectly through higher costs paid by the
consumer while a hearing drags on—were on the order of
$70,000 per day . . . [The] amounts involved supply the most
persuasive argument for taking every reasonable step to shorten
and simplify future proceedings."

Thus the litigative mode is calculated to lengthen and compli-
cate, not to shorten and simplify. The resulting high costs of ad-
judication reinforce existing inequities of power by discriminat-
ing against the poor—and that is, against those whom interest
brokerage at the political level has already left least well off.
Provision for almost unlimited rights of intervention in cases by

all parties capable of demonstrating some interest in the conflict can lead to interminable delays. This gives a further edge to wealthy corporations with the greatest staying power.

Unhurried review of evidence surely helps secure the rights of all parties. But there is no guarantee that the right evidence will be presented. There exists even less reason to suppose that lawyers and judges are most competent to review it.

Any important case is liable to further review by an appellate court. Judicial review is an important (albeit an expensive and time-consuming) procedure to protect rights. Yet this procedure reinforces lawyers' reluctance to offer arguments which do not already have standing in the judicial precedents against which appealed decisions are likely to be tested. Forums dominated by legalism—and by legal jargon and doctrine—have proved unreceptive to the kinds of statistical data and sophisticated econometric analyses likely to be crucial for sound energy policy. So process controls substance; quality in decisionmaking may yield to inappropriate procedures for selecting, presenting, and evaluating data; the way is largely barred to testing of new doctrines at the rate made necessary by advancing technology, a deteriorating environment, and growing concern about the adequacy of energy supplies.

For a variety of reasons, therefore, the litigative process hardly permits—let alone encourages—forthright, flexible, and innovative representation of the public interest. Management of energy resources in the public interest would seem to require a more explicitly executive, planning orientation—perhaps, as already suggested, based in one executive department, or maybe initially in a multi-agency program directed from the White House staff.

Back to Economics. The political-regulatory structure and legal redress offer useful mechanisms for marginal adjustments in energy policy. But despairing of the market—still the primary American allocative mechanism—and putting primary reliance on secondary and tertiary fallback systems offers little hope of a comprehensive solution. Neither the political process, nor administrative rulemaking, nor court decisions offer the possibilities for efficient decentralized decisionmaking that a smoothly functioning market can.

Litigation redistributes costs remedially—in particular cases, after the harm has occurred. The political-regulatory apparatus operates prospectively and categorically. Thus a political body can legislate an acceptable level of air quality or liquid effluent discharge for an entire region. But then costly machinery for inspection, enforcement, and punishment must be set in motion. Such schemes invite evasion if the entrepreneur thinks he can get away with it, for full compliance under any policed system always adds to costs. The preferable situation is one in which economic incentive, rather than threat of punishment, furnishes the main enforcement mechanism. How might such a mechanism work?

For a given locale, studies could estimate the ecosystem's absorptive capacity for different effluents. Then a fee schedule might be set for different levels of discharge of the residues likely to be vented in that region. These fees would be calibrated to the degree of environmental harm—seral disturbance, pollutive build-up, and maybe even depletive waste—anticipated at the various discharge levels. At any level of discharge, the appropriate effluent fees would be paid by the potential polluter for use of the environment as a coupling medium or assimilative sink. Collected fees could defray the cost of restoring the affected ecosystem through public works programs. By an effluent fee system, nature, long considered a "public good," would be appropriated to the public domain. In the public interest, its free private use would be denied to "interested publics," whether individual or industrial.

Alternatively, instead of paying the fees, the wastemaker could elect to upgrade his own effluent-control capability. The right fee schedule would put each polluter under an incentive to do so—hence improving the nation's energy order by private action—so long as control costs at a given level of waste creation are less than the fee for venting those wastes.

Such a system decentralizes decisionmaking, preserves individual choice, stimulates initiative by rewarding more efficient control technology, and looks ultimately to self-enforcement of efforts for environmental quality.

Economic incentive links private action with the public goal of ecological restoration. Once the system is in operation, and each producer knows his fees and upgrading costs, the regula-

tory authorities need only inspect and collect bills. Private decisionmakers' profit calculations will determine the size of these
bills on the basis of an "effluent fee versus upgrading cost" com-
parison. But whatever fees are actually paid will meet the need,
provided they have been precomputed to cover environmental
restoration still needed *after* the firm has responded to the fee
system's built-in incentives by improving its own effluent control
capacity.

Effluent fees would not altogether "eliminate the negative."
They explicitly envision some continued use of the environment's assimilative capacities. But the fee system idea does seek
to harmonize the economic with the ecological facts of life. It
would attempt in each locale to maximize the good side of energy use, while explicitly recognizing and managing the "bads"
using a wide range of techniques.

The Data Base: A Question of Questionable Numbers

The effluent-fee principle is widely accepted by economists. The
working market needed to execute such a system is in being, as
is the governmental machinery needed for monitoring and fee-
processing. Not now available—and most needed—is the right
technological and ecological data, developed from a common
format but collected on a region-by-region (or even an ecosys-
tem-by-ecosystem) basis.

For each locale, finding the optimum ecosystem-economy interface is a task of empirical science, not one of abstract economic theory or ecological purism.

Indeed, dissolved is any hard distinction between the artificial
and the natural, between the energy order and the ecosystem as
complementary effluent control devices in a single system. Dissolved too is the dichotomy between absolute suppression of effluents, and their venting regardless of local assimilative capacities. The redistributive imperative requires a mix of abatement
and segregation techniques, *plus* techniques to control some residues for recycling, *plus* techniques to vent wastes in suitable
amounts for dispersion or degradation. Continuous collection of
data on results will be needed, and the mix varied accordingly.
Pragmatism should guide policy.

The frontier American traditionally saw environmental quality as a non-problem, a non-question. Then in the 1960's, environmental policy became a doctrinaire question—a matter of "eco-theology," much of whose substantive content consisted of apocalyptic prophecies and chantings to "Mother Earth." In fact, environmental quality *is* an issue, and a very practical one. It depends on the location and the degree of free venting of specific wastes, both of which are empirical questions.

Industrialists may assert that subsidies are in the public interest because they lead to positive externalities vastly outweighing any negative environmental spillovers. But such assertions do not conclude the facts. Ecology lobbyists too may proclaim "inherent rights" which pollution allegedly subverts. But neither do such proclamations consider the balancing of effects which enters into an economic endeavor. Whether the balance is positive or negative is a question in each case of empirical fact. Most needed is a process, presumably initiated by government, which is optimized to deploy scientific techniques for the discovery of needed facts.

Collection of the right data in the right form presupposes an adequate research design, based on theories or "models" of the phenomena in question. Comprehensive environmental models, developed not for laboratory research but for policy-oriented data acquisition, are just coming into sight. Their elaboration—and their early use—deserves top priority on energy policymakers' agendas.

Yet a caveat is in order. It takes a hardy bureaucrat to "go quantitative." Scientific decisionmaking presumes an initial period of policy formulation in an atmosphere of uncertainty, of experimentation—and of vulnerability, owing to the inevitable primitiveness of the developing data base. At the start, any such effort draws criticism—much of it, justified. The quantitative data initially available for use in evaluating policy alternatives are inaccurate and incomplete. Undefined or questionable assumptions invariably underlie pioneering analyses. But there must be a willingness to live with such defects in the data base during the "shakedown" period of a new decisionmaking regime. Otherwise policymaking based on scientific data in the long run is foredoomed. For only if decisions actually are made on the basis of whatever data are available—as an earnest that

analysis and data *are* important—will those involved in the operations under study, whether public or private, have any incentive to gather the needed information.

Data get improved only if they are used. Thus it is a caution
of despair to let the need for improvement prevent their being
used in the first place.

Still in all, even surpassingly coarse quantitative estimates can
prove surprisingly valuable. The energy-environment interaction
defines a brand new policy field. In such a field, data which give
so much as an order-of-magnitude sense of problems may represent a substantial improvement over the existing state of knowledge. The setting of national policy properly begins with the
setting of priorities. Often, even crude quantitative knowledge of
problems that need the most urgent and concerted attention is
preferable to ignorance masquerading as a qualitative "sense of
the problem."

For example, on the basis of journalistic reports, the typical
politically literate citizen would probably focus on offshore
blowouts or tanker spills as the area of oil industry operation
most needing corrective legislation. In fact, quite the opposite
seems true on the basis of exceedingly rough quantitative data.

Thus indirect subsidies, in the form of import restrictions on
trade in cheap foreign oil, cause much more serious distortions
of true oil costs than do polluting seeps or spills. Walter Mead,
the economist who estimated the Santa Barbara blowout's external costs at $5.4 million, set the yearly social cost of oil import
restrictions at $4 billion. And a 1969 study for the President's
Oil Import Task Force estimated the social cost of import quotas at close to $7 billion annually. To these figures must be
added the costs of depletion allowances. Even under a reduced
22½% Federal depletion deduction established for oil and gas in
1970, petroleum producers as a clear "special interest" can, over
time, recover several times the actual cost of finding new
reserves—but at substantial cost to the general public. Losses to
the Treasury as a result of all mineral depletion allowances have
been estimated at between $80 to $200 million in World War II;
at up to half a billion in 1950; and at close to $4.5 billion in
1962, some $2.3 billion of which stemmed from lost revenues to
oil and gas depletion.

Despite the obvious differences between fiscal subsidies and oil-associated ecosystem degradation, the two categories have this in common: They both distort the workings of the market, and understate the true costs of oil to the citizen's disadvantage. Of highest significance is the extent of the distortion in each case. Oil spills represent a miniscule cost category compared with the social burden of other features of the oil industry. But in an ecologically conscious era, subsidies to mammoth corporations draw not nearly so much informed, or impassioned, public attention as do occasional kills of seabirds or kelp beds.

Needed in this as in other energy areas, is a sustained program —a program with credibility and high-level official backing—to acquire, analyze, and disseminate the needed ecological data. Such data would have a three-fold payoff. *First,* they could be used throughout government to help determine in a given locale the effects of controlling energy-associated effluents, as against relying on the ecosystem's self-cleansing capacities to consume wastes that may be freely vented. *Second,* and following from the first, effluent fee schedules could be drawn up on the basis of such data. *Third,* the data could assist in litigative processes when use of the judicial fallback seemed indicated. "Judicial notice" might be taken of such data, not only in courts but by Federal and state regulatory agencies as well, provided that they were standardized and collected in such a manner as to insure their credibility.

In other words, standardization of the data base for all official energy-environment decisionmaking would help overcome the fragmentation of energy-environment policy by insuring at least that official planners and regulators proceed from a common stipulation of the facts.

Summary: Beyond the Ecological Perspective

From profligate resource exploitation under America's frontier ethic, to the contemporary polarization of "economic growth" proponents versus ecological activists, substitution of inadequate theory for attention to empirical fact has hampered the evolution of a sound energy policy. An optimistic economic doctrine opened all eyes to the "goods" of rapid industrial expansion, just as it closed them to the "bads." Thus where American energy policy has failed, it has failed from sheer misperception of the facts. The facts are that externalities build up on the negative as well as on the positive side of the economic equation. Competition among firms can lead to the cutting of costs below the threshold needed to repair environmental harm, as readily as it leads to technological innovation. Environmental diseconomies and depletions may increase apace with desirable economies of larger-scale operations—though traditional energy industry practice emphasized only the positive side. Air pollutants agglomerate in a localized urban ecosystem as a result of industrial concentration, right along with a trained labor force and the technological infrastructure. In each of these respects, there is as compelling a public interest in "eliminating the negative" as in "accentuating the positive."

Specifically, an ecological perspective is needed to liberate American energy policy from thralldom to the doctrine of pecuniary price, at least insofar as that doctrine tends to understate negative externalities. But it is just as important to have perspective as to be "ecological." Economic enterprise uninformed by a sense of environmental decency has surely led to misallocation of resources—in particular, to a squandering of such public goods as clean air and pure water. On the other hand, slavish adherence to doctrinaire canons of environmental purism leads to equally serious misallocations.

The nation would hardly be served by a huge diversion of resources from urgent needs such as urban repair and nationwide improved nutrition, for only marginal environmental gains.

Despite past market failures, the answer to bad economic practice is not "no economics" but good economics—as exemplified by cost-internalization programs implemented through effluent fees. Internalizing an erstwhile external cost shifts the burden from "innocent" parties to the purchasing consumer who is ultimately responsible for its occurrence. When such internalization is accomplished by installing new control technology, the dollar cost of energy increases—as, of course, does the price of energy in the market. Thus internalization changes a nonpecuniary externality (such as Appalachian land degradation, or health impairment by air pollution) into a pecuniary increment to price. This increment covers the cost of improving the "energy order." Such damage prevention is normally cheaper in real terms than is the ecological harm which corrective technology prevents. (See, for example, Table 7.) Therefore, internalization not only facilitates the working of the market by making true costs more nearly explicit in dollar terms, but also reduces the aggregate costs of energy.

Contemporary writings abo at the environment tend to be dramatic or romantic. While literary "meetings with the archdruid" and "blueprints for survival" focus attention on crucial issues, they provide neither perspective for analysis nor frameworks for policy. A view of environmental problems that is both balanced and critical must follow from an assessment of national energy requirements, and the effects of the resulting production on the economy. This first need is for reliable empirical data about energy sources and ecological effects, varying from oil spills to radiation.

This study, though quantitative where possible, is mainly conceptual. It suggests an ecological framework within which to view the processes channeling effluents, either through the artificial energy order, or through natural transport media and ecological sinks. These processes assign characteristics to particular energy forms: the localized destruction of coal extraction, the breakdown of the energy order in oil spills, the danger that man himself will become the sink for radiation from nuclear energy. The most immediate problems appear soluble through physical redistribution of wastes. Admittedly, technology offers but short-run solutions. But then, man most needs a more liveable environment now, from which to ponder the challenge of survival in the long run.

REFERENCES

The chapter epigraph comes from pp. 328–29 of the Lockard book (1971). The facts surrounding the Buffalo Creek disaster are taken from 21 *Coal Patrol* (March 1, 1972), furnished by Appalachian Information, Inc., of Washington, D.C. The Brandeis quote comes from *New State Ice* v. *Liebmann*, 285 U.S. 262.

The Lockard text covers the "interest broker" model of American politics, as do:

1. Arthur F. Bentley, *The Process of Government* (1908);
2. David Truman, *The Government Process* (1951);
3. George Beam, *Usual Politics* (1970).

For the specifics of the American political system interaction with the energy industries, see:

1. Harry Caudill, *Night Comes to the Cumberlands* (1962);
2. Robert Engler, *The Politics of Oil* (1961);
3. Edwin Vennard, *Government in the Power Business* (1968).

The charters of the Environmental Quality Council and the Environmental Protection Agency are contained, along with other pertinent top-level public policy and organizational pronouncements, in *Environmental Quality: The First Annual Report of the Council on Environmental Quality* (August 1970), pp. 243 ff., esp. at pp. 286 and 306.

FPC's jurisdiction was expanded in *Phillips* v. *Wisconsin*, 347 U.S. 672. On the legalistic bias of American law, see Mason and Garvey, eds., *American Constitutional History* (1964), esp. Ch. II–IV, VI. The quotes at p. 199 come from pp. 4–6, "Report to the Executive Director by the FPC Second Round Task Force on Independent Producer Regulation," (July 10, 1967).

On the economists' cases for effluent fees, see:

1. William Baumol and Wallace Oates, "Use of Standards and Prices," 1971 *Swedish Journal of Economics* 42;
2. J. H. Dales, *Pollution, Property and Prices* (1968), Ch. VI;
3. Allan Kneese and Blair Bower, *Managing Water Quality: Economics, Technology, Institutions* (1968);
4. Edwin Mills, "Economic Incentives," in M. Goldman, *Controlling Pollution* (1967).

The Mead import quota cost estimates appeared in the February 27, 1971, *New York Times,* and the depletion allowance figures in an article by Ronnie Dugger, September 1969 *Atlantic*. The study cited at p. 204 was prepared by the Charles River Associates, Cambridge, Massachusetts, under OST contract and was reported in July 1969.

Appendix

~~~~~~

Ecosystem Solvency, Quasi-Consumption and Pollutive Build-Ups: A Formal Analysis of the Concepts in Chapter 3

American society is marked by a continuing "revolution of rising expectations." The resulting popular pressures for resource exploitation must be taken as a given of public policy. In such a context, the most important question that can be asked about the supporting ecosystem is not whether it has been preserved in its natural state but whether it is ecologically solvent: *Is all excess output of wastes and effluents from the "quasi-consumption" of goods put in a form capable of dissolution and incorporation in the natural cycles?*

As emphasized in Chapter 3, for an ecosystem thus to be solvent, it is necessary to downgrade it by moving farther along the stages of seral succession than would occur in the absence of the higher waste output. Generally, the higher the rate of effluence, the more extreme will be the downgrading. By the same sign, the more costly too will be efforts at environmental restoration.

The rate of effluence depends on the rate of residues output. This output of wastes is a function of aggregate demand for the fuel in question, and of the inefficiencies which prevent complete consumption in the entire sequence of energy-use processes. These dependencies suggest exploration of the pollution problem by considering the mathematical logic of the phenomenon termed "quasi-consumption."

Let e stand for the "coefficient of quasi-consumption" for a particular food or fuel, F. That is, e equals the percentage of the supplied fuel (by weight or volume, or any other meaningful measure chosen by the analyst) which is actually "disposed of" by the consumer. Such full disposition or complete consumption could, for purposes of the following algebraic model, include body tissue incorporation, conversion into usable heat, or even change of the resource into a form suitable for completely controlled disposal.

The remaining percent of the food or fuel, signified therefore by F $(1-e)$, must be discharged into the ambient reservoirs as incompletely controlled effluents, E. These discharges are the ultimate source of environmental contaminants or pollutants, P. F, E, and P are all measured as magnitudes in some chosen time period, such as a day or a year. But the time period is not itself contained in the terms.

Some portion of these effluents will be absorbed by and assimilated into the natural ecocycles. But suppose the total quantity of wastes discharged across the economy-ecosystem interface exceeds the environment's actual assimilative capacity, signified by A_a. Then an excess of effluents, ΔE, will pollute the ecosystem. As a first approximation, pollution will be proportional to the discrepancy between the excess and the absorptive capacity. These relationships yield two basic equations:

$$(1) \qquad\qquad E = F\,(1 - e),$$

$$(2) \qquad\qquad P = \frac{\Delta E}{A_a}.$$

The total amount of a given fuel produced for eventual conversion, F, depends on the number n of potential consumers (or rather, quasi-consumers) multiplied by the average per capita demand for fuel, d. This demand equals the average per capita use of fuel which would occur if fuel were free, b, reduced by a function—assumed to be linear—giving the reduction in demand associated with increases in prices, since demand falls off as market price increases. Let price equal qC_T, where C_T is the actual total unit cost of producing and marketing the fuel, and q is a coefficient (greater than 1) adjusting cost to yield a rate of return or profit to entrepreneurs sufficient to get the demanded fuel, F, produced. Then where c is the coefficient of elasticity, defined here as the decrease in demand per unit increase in price, demand equals: $b - cqC_T$. This gives:

$$(3) \qquad\qquad F = nb - nc\,(qC_T).$$

The coefficient of quasi-consumption, e in equation (1), may be expected to decrease with an increase in the cost of consumption, C, in the same way that demand slackens with increases in total cost. This assumes that increasing the efficiency of extraction and conversion, or installation of better waste-control devices, will add to the expense of using energy. Thus, a power plant operator subject to tight anti-pollution laws may have to pay an increment for abatement technology above the market price of fuel, C_T, effectively increasing his cost of primary energy. But in the absence of mandatory abatement, the likelihood that such an operator will bother to insure more nearly complete conversion or control will decrease with his perception that such efforts must increase the costliness of his operation. That is, e varies inversely—and again, it is assumed for simplification, linearly—with C.

If m gives the rate of this decrease, then: $e = 1 - m$ C. (The ordinal intercept of this linear equation for e equals 1 on the assumption that consumption would be complete—no residues vented to the environment—if perfect pollution-control were free, that is, if C were equal to zero.) Substituting this expression for e in equation (1) yields:

$$(4) \qquad\qquad E = F\ (mC).$$

This accords with the commonsense expectation that uncontrolled effluents tend to increase with the quantity of fuel consumed and with the costs of more nearly approaching complete consumption or waste control.

As vented effluents increase, the absorptive capacity of the environment required, A_r, will also increase. This increase will be proportional to the added assimilative or "ecological solvent" requirements which result from each unit increase in E.

The kind and quantity of solvent units required for natural assimilation of residues will vary with the effluent or waste-form. For example, in the case of human wastes, acid drainage from coal mines, and excess heat from central electric power plants, the usual assimilant or dissipant is water. But for each of these waste forms, the required number of "solvent units" will differ. One kind of refuse may require a large volume of water acting over a long period of time to assimilate the waste; another form, the same volume acting over a shorter period; still a third, a different volume and different time period. A solvent unit does not, then, refer to some fixed physical substance acting at a specific rate. Rather, this concept can have a wide range of referents depending on the effluent in question. It is, moreover, equally applicable to environmental reservoirs (such as air and soil) other than water. A *"solvent unit" is whatever magnitude of the appropriate natural solvent or assimilative medium per unit time must be made available ecologically to take up a single unit (usually by volume or weight) of the waste-form in question.*

Let S signify this solvent requirement for one residue of a fuel, such as sulfur dioxide from coal-burning or CO from gasoline combustion. (Throughout this model, use of an *italicized capital* will serve as reminder that the term does not measure a scalar quantity but a rate at which the resource must be made available per unit time.) Then at any given level of effluent output at a specific point of discharge, given by equation (4), it follows that:

(5) $A_r = E(S).$

The interesting problem emerges when there are disparities between the required and the actual assimilative capacities of the environment—between A_r above and A_a from equation (2).

Assume that a local ecosystem in its natural state can make available quantity K of the appropriate solvent or dilutant for a given effluent at its point of discharge. Thus K is the upper limit of the environment's absorptive capacity for the waste in question. But the actual assimilative capacity of the ecosystem will fall below K by amounts associated with any interferences with this natural limit. And, indeed, certain human uses of the environment do preempt portions of the ecosystem's undisturbed ability to assimilate effluents. Three kinds of preemptive demands on the environment are readily distinguished: *human habitation* itself; depletion of reservoir capacity through *productive enterprise;* and degradation through build-ups of *pollutive waste.*

Not all of K can be used to dissipate refuse because human organisms themselves, irrespective of the sink problems in a high demand fuel economy, require the availability at certain minimum rates of air to breathe, land to live on, and water as a universal substratum of life. So from K must be deducted an amount $n(Q/n)$, where Q/n gives the per capita reduction in the solvent potential or "carrying capacity" of the environment occasioned by the biological demands of n human organisms. The remainder left by this deduction measures, so to speak, man's local "ecological fisc"—the environmental drawing account on which he must rely, while producing all the forms of energy he demands to sustain him, to absorb the refuse of his incomplete consumption. Let $K - n(Q/n) = D.$

The ecosystem's assimilative capacity, D, that is available to absorb refuse and waste will be further reduced as more and more of the absorptive potential of the environment is taken for productive uses—for "productive preemption."

It is these productive uses which yield the high energy-equivalent output that rising demand requires. Thus, the total acreage available for garbage dumps is reduced at least by the amount of land preempted in the immediate area to cultivate crops—crops being a form of "F" in equation (3), a portion of which will end up as the garbage or "E" in equation (4) that needs eventual assimilation. Productive preemption is a major problem in the disposition of earth waste piling up near coal mines. (See Chapter 4.) Again, when cooling water is taken from a stream by a power plant, it is temporarily preempted as an environmental assimilant of outfall heated water by being used in the actual production of electric power.

Therefore a further term, $F(R)$, must be subtracted from D, where R is the rate at which potential solvent units are preempted by productive uses (and hence are no longer available to assimilate a given effluent) per unit of the fuel, F, in question. Realistically, of course, the availability of solvent units for a given effluent depends on the preemptive effect of all fuels, not merely the one responsible for the waste-form in question. Thus water for mixing with a power plant outfall may be preempted in ways other than withdrawal for cooling the condenser of the plant in question. It may, for example, be preempted for consumptive use at a refinery to produce gasoline—another fuel form. So the general form of the model would deduct $F \Sigma(R)$ to cover the preemptive effect of all kinds of energy production in the neighborhood of the discharge.

What if D, minus the "productive preemption" of potential environmental solvent units given by $F(R)$, is less than A_r? Then ΔE in equation (2) will take on a positive value. In the presence of the resulting contaminant build-up in the locale, then, an already insufficiently assimilative environment will suffer further deterioration through pollution, P, from equation (2). But a pollutive build-up compounds the deficit of environmental solvent units indicated by $A_r < A_a$ in a different way from "productive preemption."

$F(R)$ merely deducts from the total capacity of the environment to take up effluents into the ecological cycles. Productive preemption reduces capacity without interfering with the workings of the ecosystem itself. But pollution includes excess effluents in its very terms. Pollution is a kind of ecosystem "signal" that the solvent cycles are overloaded. This signal feeds back into the system, further reducing absorptive capacity, with the effect of worsening the ecosystem's assimilative problem even in the absence of any change in demand for fuel. The model of a polluted system is thus said to be "recursive," since one of its output terms "runs back" as an amplifying input to the degradative process. This gives pollutive build-up a self-compounding, dynamic characteristic. Rather than simply subtracting from the environment's sink capacity, pollution progressively reduces the ecosystem's ability to make solvent units available in successive time periods. Thus where dS/dt stands for the "deceleration" (or *second derivative* with respect to time) of the amount of solvent needed to assimilate a given quantity of effluent per unit of excess waste, resulting from the excess effluent,

$$(6) \qquad A_a = D - F(R) - P\left(\frac{dS}{dt}\right).$$

It would be helpful to know certain characteristics of a system proceeding in perfect ecological balance as defined in Chapter 3, with all wastes being taken up in on-going cycles at rates needed to maintain a self-cleaning steady-state.

Effluence, E, would not necessarily disappear in such an ecosystem. But ΔE *would* equal zero, meaning that A_a would just match A_r. Equating equation (5) to equation (6) and solving for E in terms of F gives:

$$(7) \qquad E = \left(\frac{D}{S}\right) - F\left(\frac{R}{S}\right) ,$$

which is the linear equation of negative slope in Fig. 18. Since in this perfectly balanced ecosystem, there, by definition, is no pollution, all terms multiplied by P drop out of equation (7).

Any combination of F and E—that is, any level of quasi-consumption of fuel with an output of effluents as given in equation (4)— which falls on the downward-sloping straight line of Fig. 18 will exactly exhaust the assimilative capacities of the environment. *Ecosystem solvency requires only an F-E combination lying on or beneath the downward-sloping line.* Any combination falling beneath this line will leave some excess absorptive or dilutive capacity. Then

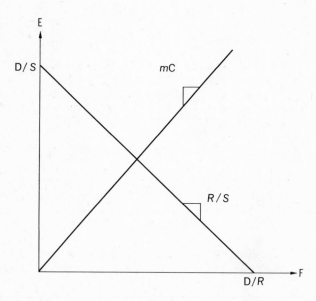

FIGURE 18
Energy-Associated Effluents as a Function of Fuel Used

it will be possible to increase demand for (or quasi-consumption of) the fuel in question, with resulting increases in effluents, up to a level where the F-E combination falls on the line. An ecosystem conforming to these descriptions may be termed solvent.

However, the relationships between F, E, and mC, or consumer response to changes in the cost of more or less complete consumption—above all, the cost of effluent control devices having the effect of increasing consumption of input fuel—will further restrict the actual patterns of quasi-consumption. A plot of equation (4) gives the line of positive slope in Fig. 18. A system, to be in ecological balance, *can* lie anywhere on the downward-sloping line. But a system *will*, in accordance with the logic of equations (1-4), have an F-E combination as indicated by the intersection of the two functions in Fig. 18. Here the value of E which just produces a "balance" with the environment's absorptive capacities—that is, E_b—is given by:

$$(8) \qquad E_b = \left[\frac{D}{S + (R/mC)} \right],$$

obtained by substituting equation (4) for F in equation (7), and then solving for E.

Now consider an ecosystem of endangered solvency, in which effluents exceed the value of E_b. Then P in equation (6) will be positive. A_r will exceed A_a. And ΔE will be given by subtracting equation (8) from equation (4);

$$(9) \qquad \Delta E = \frac{F(mC)\, S + F\,(R) - D}{S + (R/mC)}.$$

The relationship between the amount of F demanded and the level of pollution which results can be derived by substituting equations (6) and (9) into equation (2) and simplifying:

$$(10) \qquad F = \frac{1}{mC + PR} \left[- P^2 \left(\frac{dS}{dt} \right) + P(D) + \frac{D}{S + R/mC} \right].$$

Equation (10) assumes that for the level of F considered in a given ecosystem bounded in space and time, empirical determination can fix constant values for dS/dt, S and R, for mC, and for D.

Equations (2), (6), and (10) suggest the usefulness of cybernetic models in the analysis of the environmental effects of energy demand and quasi-consumption. The cybernetic concept of positive feedback is especially pertinent, for an ecosystem burdened by excess effluence contains information, in the form of pollution, which cycles back and influences subsequent stages in the system's history. In such circumstances an increase in demand for energy in any form tends both to increase wastes in accord with equation (4), and to reduce the ability of the ambient reservoirs to absorb excess wastes, as in equation (6). Worsening degradation will result unless some of the increased output is dedicated to the task of somehow enlarging the environment's absorptive capacity (e.g., developing better residue controls or better ecosystem couplings).

The crucial requirement for ecological solvency, then, is not that there be no artificial effluence. Most important from the ecosystem's standpoint is that the rate at which refuse is discharged into natural transport media and sinks not exceed for each effluent the rate at which absorption is possible. Put differently, an ecosystem will be balanced when the available solvent units equal the reciprocal of the unit measure of pollution for each potential pollutant:

$$(11) \qquad\qquad\qquad P \times S = 1.$$

Then the effluent gets assimilated at a rate which equals its discharge. Thus the product of P, or quantity of excess contaminats per available solvent units, and S, or the rate at which the given effluent must be taken up in order to keep an ecological steady-state, may be used as a rough index of the load on the system. Any time the system becomes overloaded,

$$(12) \qquad\qquad P\,(S) > 1 = \text{``Pollution Index.''}$$

This concept emphasizes that pollution is not necessarily most meaningfully measured in terms of physical parts of a contaminant per unit of air or water. The pollution index—whose determination presumes numerical solution of P in equation (10) for a given level of fuel—rather emphasizes the rate of overrun of waste output beyond the ecosystem's capacity to cleanse itself. While in no way excluding consideration of pecuniary cost, estimation of the terms in equation (10) for various fuels under different ecological conditions can help give a feel for the ecosystem costs of pollution.

Glossary

<hr style="border-style: dashed" />

Technical terms and neologisms are listed alphabetically and in capital letters. All italicized terms in the definitions are themselves defined elsewhere in the glossary.

BIODEGRADATION: *Ecological consumption* by living organisms, in which the matter being degraded serves as food for the degrading agents.

BIOMASS: Living matter. All biomass produced by *photosynthesis* is called "primary." Secondary biomass consists of all living matter which takes energy from metabolizing primary biomass—that is, the body tissue of herbivores and certain parasitic plants.

BRITISH THERMAL UNIT (Btu): The quantity of heat needed to raise 1 pound of water through 1 degree Fahrenheit.

CONCENTRATION, STRATEGY OF: Any scheme for environmental quality which seeks to concentrate wastes in the *energy order* to increase their ease of handling and control, as for more secure disposal in areas which are segregated from life forms. Contrasted with the *strategy of dispersal.*

CONSUMPTION, ECOLOGICAL: The process by which any substance is degraded from a higher- to a lower-energy state, or broken down from an existing physical configuration to less complex elements, with energy in the form of heat released in the process. Most commonly, ecological consumption occurs through the metabolic or respiratory process of oxidation (i.e., "burning").

COUPLING, ECOLOGICAL: Any means, whether natural or artificial, whereby matter in one ecosystem may be transported to a second ecosystem. In the desirable case, the second ecosystem has excess assimilative capacity. Thus it can absorb or *ecologically consume* the transported matter without harm. In the undesirable case, the coupled ecosystem itself becomes *polluted,* or suffers undue *seral disturbance,* as a result of the input of the matter.

DEPLETIVE WASTE: That portion of the *energetic cost* of fuel production or conversion which results from inefficiency in the procedures or the technology used to exploit the resource in question.

DISPERSION, STRATEGY OF: Any scheme for improving the habitability of the environment by dispersing and diluting potentially harmful effluents in order to reduce their concentrations below some threshold at which they will do harm if they come into contact with a living organism.

ECOSYSTEM: A self-sustaining community of organisms together with the community's physical locale, usually contrasted both with human society and with artificial man-made structures. ("The ecosystem" is also used to refer to the natural environment generally. In the foregoing pages, the context makes clear which usage is intended whenever the word is used.)

ECOSYSTEM-ECONOMY INTERFACE: The boundary at which human control through the *energy order* of a given resource or its associated wastes either starts (i.e., the point at which extractive technology moves the resource out of its raw state in nature) or ends (i.e., the point at which a fuel or an effluent is vented to a *receiving ecosystem* for ultimate *ecological consumption*).

ENERGETIC COST: All inputs of energy in any form (e.g., solar energy, or past geological pressures exerted on decaying vegetation to form coal), whether provided by man or by nature, which have gone into the production of given resource, and which are rendered unrecoverable—whether for thermodynamic, economic, or engineering reasons—in the course of human exploitation of that resource.

ENERGY ORDER: The entire man-made physical apparatus used to control the location, concentration, and movement of fuels and fuel-associated effluents.

EUTROPHICATION: The process by which an ecosystem ages. Generally used in reference to aquatic ecosystems that are over-rich in nutrients, with a resulting high rate of *ecological consumption* of energetically charged matter, and general degradation of the locale's aesthetic and economic value to humans.

FISSION, NUCLEAR: The splitting of atomic nuclei (generally of particular isotopes of "heavy" elements, such as uranium and plutonium), accompanied by the release of heat. Nuclear reactors of current and foreseeable design, including breeder reactors, generate heat by controlled fission.

FUSION, THERMONUCLEAR: The process by which atomic nuclei (generally of "light" elements, such as hydrogen and deuterium) join together, accompanied by the release of heat. Hydrogen bombs are uncontrolled fusion devices triggered by an A-bomb explosion. Controlled fusion is not yet feasible, even in the laboratory.

GENETIC DEATH: The disappearance of a detrimental gene from the gene pool of the species. Such a harmful gene reduces the biological fitness of its possessors, however slightly. Hence, over time, it causes its possessors to reproduce relatively fewer children than do non-possessors, thus gradually representing a smaller and smaller portion of the species' genetic endowment, until it vanishes.

LOCALIZATION OF EFFECTS: The phenomenon whereby inadequate ecological *coupling* media, either natural or artificial, result in vented wastes' accumulating in the locale where they are vented, rather than being carried off and dispersed.

MARKET: Any place or institutionalized arrangement whereby goods and services are exchanged as a result of trading by buyers and sellers.

PECUNIARY PRICE: The price of an increment of a resource, expressed in dollar terms, as set by *market* conditions. More generally, "price" is the ratio at which increments of the resource can be traded for increments of other goods, with money used as the means of measuring this rate.

PHOTOSYNTHESIS: Literally, "to make by light"—and hence, the process by which green plants convert solar energy, or light from any other source, with water and carbon dioxide into new *biomass*.

POLLUTION (or "pollutive build-up"): The build-up in a given locale of wastes, residues, or effluents from any human process. If such wastes are vented to a *receiving ecosystem* (or carried through a *coupling* mechanism to another ecosystem) in excess of the rate at which they can be naturally degraded, assimilated, or dispersed, then they will eventually accumulate to some harmful concentration.

QUASI-CONSUMPTION: The process whereby humans change the form of resources, reducing their economic value and creating wastes, leaving the *ecosystem* to complete the *ecological consumption* of these residues through natural assimilation or degradation.

RECEIVING ECOSYSTEM: The ecosystem to which a given waste form is freely vented—that is, freed from control by the *energy order*.

REDISTRIBUTIVE IMPERATIVE: The direction of environmental policy which is suggested by the phenomenon of *localization of effects*. Redistribution would look to means of more equitably "spreading" the costs of environmental degradation or clean-up, rather than permitting the continued primary impact of harm to fall on persons who happen to live in the *receiving ecosystem* for a given waste form.

SERAL DISTURBANCE: Any interference with the natural rate of aging in an *ecosystem* as a result of the introduction to that system of artificial contaminants. The disturbance may accelerate, retard or reverse the natural succession of biospheric communities. In common speech, the degradative accelerated aging of aquatic systems is called *eutrophication*. However, any *sere* which goes in the direction of increased energy cycled through the ecosystem per unit of time is properly termed *"eutrophication"* regardless of rate.

SERE: The sequence by which biospheric communities naturally succeed one another in an ecosystem at the system ages. As aging occurs, the structure and the nature of the organisms comprising the ecosystem change in a way that tends toward increased rates of *ecological production* and *consumption*.

SINK, ECOLOGICAL OR ENVIRONMENTAL: A physical locale or medium where wastes accumulate and, in the desirable case, degrade into harmless forms which are assimilated into the ecosystem.

SOLVENCY, ECOSYSTEM: The situation in which the *ecosystem* has sufficient *solvent units* to take up all residues as they are vented, thus precluding any pollutant build-ups by means of *ecological consumption*.

SOLVENT UNIT: The quantity of any physical substance or medium needed to insure *ecological consumption* of a given unit of waste at the rate at which that waste is freely vented.

SPOIL: Disturbed earth left as a residue or waste of mining.

THERM: 100,000 *Btu's*.

Index

228

INDEX